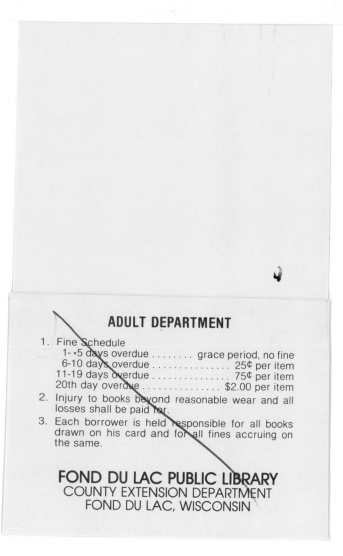

THE
PRIVATE
POLAND

THE PRIVATE POLAND

JANINE WEDEL

Facts on File Publications
New York, New York • Oxford, England

THE PRIVATE POLAND

Library of Congress Cataloging in Publication Data

Wedel, Janine
  The private Poland.

  Bibliography: p.
  Includes index.
  1. Poland—Social life and customs—1945–   .
2. Poland—Politics and government—1980–   . I. Title.
DK4442.W43   1986   943.8'05   84-24731
ISBN 0-8160-1197-4

Jacket Design: Oksana Kushnir

Printed in United States of America

10 9 8 7 6 5 4 3 2 1

To Adam, for his understanding and guidance
and
To Mama, for giving me a home

Epigraph

A Polish friend who appeared on an American news program several months after the declaration of martial law came to me troubled and upset about the interview. He was haggard, after several sleepless nights.

"If I had said that everything's fine—that I have an apartment and haven't been fired from my job—this would have left out important events, such as the arrest of my friend," he told me. "I could have said that I take packages to him in prison, but this would have made me look like a hero, and I don't want that. So in the end I said that communication between East and West is too difficult, and that there are many levels of communication. Simply, Westerners are not capable of reading between the lines. This statement can be interpreted in two ways—that translating across East-West cultural barriers is impossible and explaining the true situation in Poland is too difficult or that I'm frightened to say what I really think of the current situation. Both of these interpretations are correct."

After a long stay in Poland and intimate contacts there, I came to get a glimpse of what lies beneath the surface. As I told a Polish friend who wanted to know what I was writing about: "This book is about how I began to understand Poland."

Contents

Preface

I sang in a Polish country music group and toured the countryside, performing for and later toasting with country and town folk, who had often come to see their first American. We performed in the small town of Kęty (population 18,000), half way between Wadowice, the birthplace of Pope John Paul II, and the town of Oświęcim, in the West better known as Auschwitz. Afterwards, members of the band retired to the club with an energetic, fortyish mother—a school teacher—her two teenage daughters and the boyfriend of one of the daughters. Over beer and cherry vodka, the conversation shifted from serious to light topics—both often mixed in the same breath. They asked me lively questions about American country and English folk music traditions. They told "Russian jokes," which created the impression that the Soviet Union was, for them, an exotic place far removed from their Poland. And they also talked about realities of life at home.

The teenage boyfriend spoke of the nearby town of Oświęcim. "When Auschwitz ended, Oświęcim began," he said sadly. During the Second World War, Auschwitz was the largest of the concentration camps. Now environmentally hazardous chemical works loomed over the camp, preserved as a museum, and over the town of Oświęcim.

After our performances, I sat through countless such late-night evenings with local folk, listening to the joys and despairs of people whose concerns sometimes seemed familiar, sometimes worlds apart from those of Westerners.

Who were these people I came to know and how did they place themselves in relation to others in their society? Sixty percent of the population is urban, and my main contacts were with urbanites who reside in the larger cities of Warsaw, Cracow, Toruń, Gdańsk, Szczecin and smaller towns, such as Żyrardów, Oś-więcim and Bielsko-Biała. Many of my observations concern large cities, though I also have friends in small towns and rural villages.

I came to Poland for the first time before anyone could have imagined the emergence of Solidarity, the famous social movement. During a nine-year period, from 1977 to 1986, I have had contact with several hundred Poles.

In 1977 I travelled throughout the country and in 1979 I lived in Toruń for several months. The turbulent years of the 1980s brought me again to Poland. During my two-year stay during and after martial law, from 1982 to 1984, I conducted research for a Ph.D. dissertation in Anthropology and was associated with the Institute of Sociology at Warsaw University. From 1985 to 1986 I carried out post-doctoral research. I lived as a Pole "under the same roof and at the same table" with Polish families. I shared their joys and cares.

I moved among old and young, rich and poor, politically active and uncommitted, religious and agnostic, city dwellers and farm workers. My contacts included secretaries, bureaucrats, teachers, seamstresses, lawyers, professors, students, physicians, photographers, chemists, engineers, actors, book binders, janitors, writers, railroad conductors, plumbers and members of the armed forces. I moved among Communist Party members and members of the opposition, intellectuals and members of the working class.

There was life at the university, saturated with the

latest rumors about faculty members and students
who had just been arrested, speculation about the
next move of a particular Solidarity faction, the government or the Catholic Church, and a generally uncertain atmosphere about the future. There was life
among older friends who related stories of their past
under the German occupation, of daily fear and of
scarcity. "It's difficult for me to think of my boyhood
at night," said my journalist neighbor, as, over vodka,
he told about his childhood in a concentration camp.
There was also a day when I stood at Auschwitz with
Suzanne, my sister, who wept at the sight of children murdered in gas chambers.

☆   ☆   ☆

I learned that Poles generally say they descend from
one of these large groups: "workers," "peasants" or
"intelligentsia." Workers implies manual laborers;
peasants are usually farmers, but the term can refer
to the entire rural population. There is a traditional
definition of intelligentsia as well as a broader, postwar bureaucratic definition based on official ideology. Because this ideology was consciously designed
to eliminate opposition to the state bureaucracy, implicit in the historical definition of intelligentsia, the
new meaning includes not only the cultural elite—
comprised largely of intellectuals—but also the state
bureaucracy.

Urbanites usually consider themselves members of
the intelligentsia. Those who think of themselves as
part of the intelligentsia may refer to workers and
peasants as "simple" or "primitive" and think of
themselves as "cultured." Urbanites tend to look
down upon rural—"traditional" or "peasant"—Polish culture.

I mainly participated and observed—in contrast to
most Westerners (especially political scientists and

economists) conducting research on contemporary Poland. I did not ask people intimate questions about their lives, but they allowed me to see them operating under conditions of economic and political turmoil.

To protect Polish sources, I have created fictional characters. They are true to my observations in general. In many cases I attempted to avoid the identification and description of particular individuals. And any resemblance to actual people is purely coincidental.

I refer to some of the characters as "Pan" or "Pani" (in English Mr. or Mrs.) with an initial representing their last names (Pan B. or Pani R.). Others, I refer to by first names (Janusz or Grażyna). Still others, I refer to as "Pan" or "Pani" plus a first name (Pan Jan or Pani Elżbieta). These different titles reflect my different relationships with people, which are determined largely by age. A person of my age is usually on *ty* (familiar form) terms with other young adults once a personal relationship has been established. A younger adult addresses older adults as "Pan" or "Pani" and expects the same titles in return. If, however, a personal relationship of affection has been established, I may show this by calling the older individual "Pan Jacek" or "Pani Janina"; he or she may show affection by referring to me as *ty* and calling me by my first name.

In my three-year stay I recorded a separation between the public and the private in all aspects of the Polish world—in the ritual character of public life and the personal nature of private life. Anthropologists have traditionally studied small-scale societies or communities. Increasingly, however, they are studying the complex societies which were formerly the realm of sociologists, political scientists and economists. An ethnographic study of the interrelated private and public components of Polish life, in political, economic and social spheres, would provide insights that could not be obtained through research in a more narrowly defined discipline.

At the outset of my journey to Poland I could not have predicted specifically what I would find. It was not until I reviewed my diary after nearly six months of detailed note taking that I fully realized what I had come for.

I had had the opportunity to see the conflicts that thrash about in the minds of individuals, note how they deal with them and how they manage their day-to-day circumstances. In looking through my diary, I realized I had taken note, most of all, of people's abilities to maneuver within and outside of the system. I had seen how the private world mixes daily with the complicated world of Polish public life.

I would attempt to paint a picture of Polish society centered around day-to-day interactions. This would explain more than a pedantic, narrow disciplinary approach. Such a personal approach adds another dimension to our understanding of what has come to be known as the "Polish crisis."

Acknowledgments

I wish to thank the Fulbright program and the International Research and Exchanges Board (IREX) for giving me the opportunity to conduct research in Poland. I would like to thank the Polish Ministry of Higher Education and Warsaw University for its sponsorship of my Fulbright and IREX grants and for its cooperation in my study and fieldwork in Poland.

I wish to thank Kate Kelly, my editor, for her encouragement, spirit and fine editorial guidance, and Nancy Trichter, literary agent, for her expertise and patience in reading numerous drafts.

I am deeply indebted to many Poles—friends and acquaintances—who took it upon themselves to explain their world to me. I am especially appreciative of Professor Antoni Kamiński, Director of the Institute of Sociology, Warsaw University, Professor Mirosława Marody of Warsaw University and Adam Pomorski for having given generously of their time in guiding my research and writing. I am extremely grateful to Pani Antonina Dachów and Dr. Elżbieta Dachów-Siwiec for their warmth, kindness and generous help during my recent stay of nearly three years.

I wish to thank Jacek Łaszczuk and Andrzej Zygmuntowicz for photographs.

I am indebted to many advisors and colleagues, including Professors Aleksandra Jasińska-Kania, Witold Morawski, Stefan Nowak and Barbara Szacka, and Drs. Jolanta Babiuch, Grzegorz Lindenberg and Grażyna Kacprowicz of Warsaw University; Professors Włodzimierz Wesołowski, Edmund Mokrzycki, Joanna Kurczewska and Joanna Sikorska of the Polish Academy of Sciences; Professors Jacek Kurczewski and Krzysztof Kicinski of the Institute of Social Prevention and Resocialization; and Professor Antoni Rajkiewicz of the Ministry of Labor, Salaries and Social Policy. Some of them directed me to research conducted by Polish social scientists; others assisted me by reviewing and discussing my manuscript.

I wish to thank Drs. Jan Kordos, Władysław Kondrat and Wiesław Łagodziński of the Central Statistical Office (GUS) for helping me to complete my data.

I am grateful to countless others who, for lack of space, will remain unnamed, but who helped in numerous ways in my daily affairs and in the carrying out of my research.

I wish to express my gratitude to my advisors at the University of California, Berkeley—Professors Laura Nader, Burton Benedict and Gregory Grossman—for their careful reading and critical comments on my doctoral dissertation, which formed the conceptual framework of this book. I also wish to thank Professors Nelson Graburn, Martin Landau, Eugene Hammel, Melvin Kohn, Margaret Mackenzie and Ernest Landy for critiquing all or parts of my manuscript.

I wish to acknowledge special friends: in particular Helen Stoltzfus, who was a loyal supporter of this project and a constant source of encouragement. I wish to thank Dr. Erna P. Harris for providing numerous opportunities for free concerts and other diversions and for posing challenging questions during my fieldwork and writing. I am appreciative of Madeline Landau, Walter Cingo, Michael Steinlauf, William Harwood and Andrzej Lubowski for offering insight into the Polish situation from their own diverse experiences. I would like to express my gratitude to Carrie Doyle, Laura Fraser and Urie Bender who offered invaluable assistance in editing my work, to Rebecca Slough, for typing numerous drafts of the manuscript and to Karen Ledwin for numerous favors.

Finally, I wish to thank my family members for their generous support. I am deeply indebted to my sister, Dr. Suzanne Wedel, without whose financial assistance my research and preparation of this manuscript would have been impossible.

Given the complicated nature of the material this book deals with, it would be tempting to pass the responsibility to others. Yet while many helped, I alone am responsible for the final product.

Introduction:
A First Glimpse
of Martial Law Poland

A t 10:00 on the evening of December 12, 1981, a friend approached me at a Christmas party in Berkeley, California and said he had just heard a radio report: martial law had been declared in Poland. I hurried home to listen to the news. One by one, my Polish friends, most of them visiting scholars at the University of California, began to contact me. In despair, Marek appeared at my door. Marysia called me on the telephone, crying, "A war just started in Poland." Jacek, visiting friends in another town, also called, after downing several shots of vodka. I asked him how he was.

"I am well," he replied, "but Poland is not well."

We gathered together that first evening, still in shock. Over vodka, we voiced our worst fears, listened to the continual newsbreaks and anxiously speculated about the fate of family, friends and Poland. None of us knew what "martial law" would mean for Poland's nearly 37 million people. General Wojciech Jaruzelski had cut all communications and sealed all borders. Most of us imagined the worst— civil war, Soviet invasion or both. I suspected that, for me, this turn of events meant that my trip to Poland, scheduled for January of 1982, would be postponed, if not cancelled. All visas had been invalidated by martial law.

I spent the next two weeks exchanging news and commiserating with Polish friends in California who were worried about the fate of their families and friends. They also wondered whether they could ever return to Poland.

"I can't imagine what Christmas in Poland will be like this year," one told me quietly.

The U.S. State Department carefully monitored Soviet troop maneuvers near the Polish border. With Western reports of mass arrests and speculation of civil war or Russian invasion, Poles, alone in a foreign country, were alarmed. The attempt to assign interpretations to events seemed endless: Was the government waging a show of power with the intention of eventually negotiating with Solidarity? One friend said, "I don't know what Jaruzelski wants. What can he possibly have to offer? Who will negotiate with him now?" A student of draft age wondered if he might be interned were he to return to Poland. Would he be drafted? Had his friends been interned? Would they be drafted? A visiting physicist spoke bitterly, tears dropping into her dinner: "I think about the life of my mother—she was born in 1907. Her life has been so sad—World War I, World War II, now. Why should my mother's biggest task be to find a bar of soap?" Another woman complained that her monthly salary from the Polish Academy of Sciences was now worth only $5 and that she would have to work for months to pay the rent on the large apartment in which she lives.

Smuggled notes from family and friends in Poland served as a prime source of both information and anxiety. The news in such messages spread like wild fire within the nationwide circle of visiting professors and students. A Polish visiting scholar received a letter several days before Christmas informing him that his family of five was fine and that he "should stay in the United States longer to earn more dollars." The extra hard currency he could earn was more crucial to the family than the help he could offer in Poland.

An American professor returning from his stay at a Polish university brought news of the arrest of former colleagues. With a crowbar, police had broken the door of a woman Solidarity activist in the middle of the night. They had dragged her from her apartment and taken her to an internment camp. Her English husband had been unable to determine her whereabouts. A visiting scholar at the University of California who received a smuggled letter from her sister in Poland spoke of a "campaign of systematic terror" and loyalty oaths. The letter speculated that scholars at the university would be required to sign the oath or face being fired. "I won't sign any bloody loyalty oath," said the visiting scholar resolutely, as she wondered about the prospects of returning to her job in Poland.

The letter detailed other government tactics: the circulation of false rumors that people were being executed in internment camps, ostensibly to scare citizens into complete submission; and the printing of false underground papers in order to confuse them. And the letter contained a joke circulating in Poland at that time: "A man goes to a store and asks the clerk 'Is it true you don't have any meat today?' The clerk replies, 'Here we don't have any fish. It's next door they don't have any meat.' "

Many of the messages received did not contain such straightforward information. Vital information was conveyed through allusion. When one friend received a picture postcard from his mother saying that "Maciej and Piotr are in a sanitarium," he understood that the two had been arrested. A Polish student knew his father wanted him to remain in the United States indefinitely when the father wrote, "We hope you will enjoy your studies there until 1985 and come back to Poland with the title of professor."

But some opened letters from Poland only to find

they had been posted before martial law. I received two such Christmas cards in California in January of 1982. They were marked "uncensored"—presumably unopened. One, from a physician, read:

> I was married on 22 June 1980. We are doing not too bad because of money I earned this year in Denmark. We are leaving Poland on 7th January 1982 to Norway (3 months) and next 3 months to Sweden. After this year, we'll have to decide where to stay for the rest of life. The Polish crisis is at least for ten years.

Another friend, an economist, wrote:

> All of us in Poland are very nervous and excited. Everyday life in Poland is becoming more and more difficult, but it isn't completely disastrous as some in the West see it. I'm trying to be a future-oriented man and live with hopes. At present I'm deeply involved in the economic reforms and *Solidarność* movement. It helps me to remain in relatively good shape.

The occasional letters and eyewitness accounts were hints of a world with which I had little direct contact. I constantly wondered about the true situation in Poland.

In February I at last received a phone call informing me my visa had been granted. Few visas were granted at the time. I received one only because the terms of the Fulbright exchange program were being honored. Family and friends told me I was "crazy" to go during a time of such turbulence and scarcity. Masking their worries, some of my Polish friends said we would meet in Poland "under better circumstances."

I began to make preparations for the trip. A Polish friend accompanied me on my shopping expedition and offered suggestions for gifts. I bought coffee, batteries, soap, toothpaste, chocolate, sausages, cheese, dishcloths, perfume, tampons, panty hose, blank cassette tapes, detergent, cigarettes, toilet paper, shampoo, Kleenex, tea, vitamin pills, warm undershirts, woolen socks, appointment books, pencils with erasers, pencil sharpeners, razor blades, paper, and, for children, crayons and stuffed animals.

More pressing than stocking up on scarce supplies was gathering messages to relay for Polish friends, visiting scholars and Poles across the country who had heard I was going. "Tell my family I'm not planning to return to Poland." "Tell my daughter that I won't be able to make it to her wedding." "Please give this money to my wife and children." One brother and sister called me: "Our father died last week. Our mother is alone is Poland. We have not been able to get a message to her—please give her our condolences."

By the time I left for Poland in February, two months after the imposition of martial law, most of my Polish friends had still received no word from or about their families. Nor had the families in Poland heard from friends and relatives abroad.

A Polish travel agency in Chicago advised me that all letters taken with me to Poland would be confiscated at the border—they would be thrown out unopened since there would be no time to censor them. I spent much of my trip painstakingly reorganizing and memorizing the letters and messages and the addresses of their intended recipients.

As the plane descended and the landscape near Warsaw became visible, I wondered what was going on in the nearly closed-off country. What would I find here? How had people's lives been shaped by the famous and now illegal Solidarity movement? My impression of Poland, based on Western press reports and compounded by the fear, uncertainty and panic of Polish friends around me, was that Poles would feel totally hopeless and that everyone would be loudly supportive of Solidarity. I imagined that

chaos, helplessness and marching in the streets pre-
vailed. I thought that basic supplies and services
would be unobtainable and that there would be very
little food.

From the airplane I looked for signs of life in the
countryside and found very few—only plots of dark
grey, green and brown with a foggy mist over them.
As we approached the outskirts of the city, I saw
more traffic, though there was less movement than
I remembered during my previous visits in 1977 and
1979. I noticed military vehicles near the airport; my
aircraft seemed to be the only plane in the area. With
a dozen or so other passengers, some of whom tear-
fully took their first glimpse of a homeland under
martial law, I deplaned at the end of the runway.
We were greeted by five soldiers, who closely observed our short trek from the plane to the connec-
tion van that was to deliver us to the airport.

The airport was carefully observed and guarded.
A darkly handsome customs official with a subdued,
controlled air about him inquired as to the contents
of each of my 11 pieces of luggage. Yet the official
merely looked in my guitar case and opened the one
box I had said contained books. Matter-of-factly, he
inquired: "Polish or English books?" Trying to appear naïve I replied: "I have Polish books—a dictionary." The official took out and examined one book,
The Pity of It All, an anthropological study of geno-
cide, and indicated I could go on.

The 11 boxes which glided easily through customs
contained painstakingly gathered supplies of canned
tuna, dishcloths, toilet paper, fur-lined boots, cooking utensils and research materials—things I had
thought I would need for the year or more of my
stay. The airline check-in clerk in New York had demanded I pay $800 for overweight baggage, but I
had pleaded: "I can't send them, the borders are
closed. No mail is arriving in Poland. There's no food.

Everything I need for the next year is contained in these boxes." I paid the clerk only $100.

Polish friends at the airport laughed at the naive foreigner who was determined to have everything she needed for an entire year, and whose luggage contained many items available in Poland. They joked that I had "prepared to visit a Third World country."

Porters, recognizing me as a Westerner, were eager to carry my luggage out of the airport. They knew I had probably not yet exchanged my money for złoty and would pay them in valued hard currency. We exited the airport into the frosty February weather, and the porters quickly found a taxi driver—no doubt one who had made a prior arrangement for a share of the Western currency.

As I rode through the Warsaw streets to my destination, my first impression of martial law Poland was that it looked much like the somewhat sullen but intriguing place I had visited previously. Tall nondescript gray buildings stood next to, and across from, other tall nondescript gray buildings. All looked alike. There were department stores, government office buildings and apartment buildings with quilts and pillows airing out on balconies and windows, decorating unpainted exterior walls. I was again impressed by the lack of signs and advertising and by the modestly labeled buildings common to the Eastern bloc. In the streets there was no immediate sense of a state of emergency. Women moved busily about toting shopping bags; children followed. People shuffled about expressionlessly, stoically looking down. Poland looked much as it had during my last visit—but now the rules were different.

In the first few hours of my stay in Poland, my Polish "mama" gave me strict instructions about my conduct. Curfew was top priority. In my diary I wrote, "Curfew is at 11:00 every night, and Mama wants me to be back at 10:00. No later." Mama asked me if

I knew that there was now a war. Martial law, as we
called it in the United States, was referred to in Poland as "state of war" or, more commonly, as "the
war."

I asked about telephone communications. They had
been restored within cities several weeks earlier, but
it remained difficult to place intercity calls. One had
to reach the operator, and only hours later might it
be possible to get a call through.

I also learned quickly that telephone conversations
are bugged. From the time a call is dialed until the
party answers, an official-sounding recorded female
voice repeats over and over again, "This conversation is monitored; this conversation is monitored; this
conversation is monitored." The voice is nasal, crisp,
irritating. It is another reminder: remember martial
law. A friend advised me how to conduct myself on
the phone: "You can talk about the weather or your
health. You can arrange to meet for coffee, vodka or
a party. But don't go far beyond these limits." She
said she knew a man occasionally listened to her
telephone conversations because he sometimes interrupted and talked with her. "Once he told me he
likes me and that he won't take any action against
me," she reported.

Politics was the subject of even the first few minutes of conversation with old friends. "Do you like
Reagan? Do you agree with his economic sanctions?"
One friend was disappointed to learn I thought Reagan's policies with respect to Poland were designed
mainly to increase his popularity at home.

"Now there are not so many organized activities
opposing the government," said an acquaintance
confidently, "but wait until the spring. The underground is growing and will continue to grow." Massive unrest seemed to be brewing. There was one
topic of conversation and one subject for graffiti artists: "The winter may be yours, but the spring belongs to us," appeared etched on city walls and un-

derpasses. No one knew exactly what the coming months would bring.

I had arrived in Poland not only with 11 suitcases of supplies and a bundle of messages but also with the mental "baggage" of Western press reports—stories of starvation, imminent civil war or Soviet invasion and political prisoners transported to the Soviet Union for punishment. Poles in the United States had been almost hysterical as they tried to guess what would happen in their homeland. Yet, as one friend put it, "Martial law was relatively bloodless. People only lost their last hope." The general mood in Poland was one of stern stoicism. The situation was uncertain, but civil war had not broken out—at least not yet. Unaware of the extent of Western press coverage of dramatic events in Poland, many Poles were surprised at the messages they received from alarmed friends and family abroad. The situation was in fact menacing, but different than one could have imagined from the West.

My first weeks were consumed by delivering messages. In a country where many people do not have telephones—and telephone communication is both unreliable and risky—I spent many hours trying to make contact. When I succeeded, there were exhausting, tearful meetings at which I tried to assure friends and family members of the well-being of loved ones abroad. In appreciation for my messages, and with the hospitality reserved for foreigners, families coaxed me to share their vodka, coffee, tea, meat and chocolate—goods supposedly in short supply.

In order to deliver a message to the fiance of a Polish woman friend in California, I had to go through a woman in Warsaw. Her son knew the fiance, who was the son of a high-ranking army officer. The woman feared his father's position might have been in jeopardy had I, an American, made direct contact. The officer's house was watched, his telephone bugged.

The curfew made evenings short, so I took a taxi when delivering one of the earliest messages. The numbering system in Polish neighborhoods is sometimes difficult to make out, so the taxi driver had to help me find the building by driving through a huge complex of tall buildings interspersed with overgrown grass, puddles of water and playground equipment. I saw no stores or businesses—only rows of buildings. Even after arrival at the correct block, the driver took 20 minutes to locate the right building. The wife of my friend in California had warned me over the telephone that there would be no electricity in the corridors or in the elevators. I had to use a flashlight to find the right apartment. When I arrived, the woman explained that, on the rare occasions when a lightbulb or battery was installed, people stole it immediately, due to shortages. She told me how she first learned about "the war" on December 13. She heard some rumblings on the radio but did not pay much attention, since she was accustomed to ignoring government rhetoric. She tried to call her mother, and the telephone was dead. But it was not until she looked out the window and saw tanks that she knew what had happened. This woman, like many of the people I met who had friends and relatives outside the country, was tremendously frustrated at being unable to make contact abroad. She was eager to relate the eventful, often traumatic stories of the preceding two months.

It seemed as if everyone actually thought relatives and friends in the States had not written them letters, simply because no letters had arrived. Of course, friends were writing diligently. Many in Poland asked me to explain the desperation expressed in smuggled messages and two-month-old letters that arrived from the West—a desperation not warranted by day-to-day reality under martial law. Throughout my stay, when I read the Western press and saw TV

footage in the American Embassy in Warsaw, I felt
as if I were living in a different country than the one
described in the news. I was surprised by the relative normality of the food situation, which had improved under martial law. Yellow cheese appeared
on the market for the first time in months, and there
was speculation that the government had been
hoarding food and goods before martial law was imposed. A rationing system ensured that everyone had
access to minimal foodstuffs and supplies. My ration
cards, those of a single person who is not a physical
laborer, included the following allotments for one
month:

Meat	2,500	g (5.5 lbs)
Butter	500	g (1.1 lbs)
Sugar	250	g & 1.5 kg (3.8 lbs)
Cigarettes	12	packages
Soap	1	bar
Alcohol	1	bottle
Flour	1	kg (2.2 lbs)
Oil or lard	0.5	kg (1.1 lbs)
Dish detergent	300	g (10 ozs)

Many Poles were amused by the contents of relief
packages from Western friends, relatives and church
and government agencies. Hoping to find luxury
items such as coffee and chocolate, one friend un-
wrapped his package from a total stranger in Came-
roon only to find flour, macaroni and other staples
plentiful in Polish stores.

Though the worst scenarios of martial law had not
come to pass, the Polish population was left almost
in the dark as to its future. The mood in Poland,
especially during the first few months, was overwhelmingly one of despair and uncertainty. As we
rode a bus through the dim and subdued city, the
elderly mother of a friend in the States remarked that
the Second World War was better than these days:

"At least *then* we had hope. I myself will not see the situation change. It is possible that my grandchildren will."

Many Poles I spoke to were convinced that the next few years would see the outbreak of conventional war in Europe. One, who voiced anti-government sentiments, detailed the following scenario in February of 1982: "There will be a war in Europe in the late summer or early fall. The Russians will start a war, moving troops all the way to Paris. The West will have no military response." I argued that Soviet invasion was highly improbable. But he persisted: "The declaration of martial law makes no sense unless the Russians wanted to tighten the reigns on Poland in preparation for a war."

The latest political rumors about the government gave birth to many fearsome predictions. Doomsday prognoses about the future abounded, and new rumors spawned even more rumors. People constantly talked politics and speculated about the future; they ate their "last piece of cake" and bought their "last bottle of alcohol."

The authorities did not use the new martial law regulations indiscriminately, yet the constitution had been amended in such a way that the powers of the state were absolute, as in a country during wartime. Many citizens felt uprooted, not because they had actually lost their jobs or because boarders were assigned to their apartments, but because they knew they could be fired or assigned lodgers to already-cramped quarters at any time.

Though the government emphasized a gradual return to normalcy—lifting the curfew, releasing many political prisoners, and diminishing police presence—it would, often without notice, institute disruptive new policies and carry out purges against various groups. The underground began to organize itself after the initial shock; opposition leaders, journalists and writers were in constant danger.

I was hosted by the Institute of Sociology at Warsaw University, and, through most of my stay, there was discussion and uncertainty about the future of social sciences and humanities institutes. Scholars were at the mercy of the government, as was everyone else. Scholars from the Polish Academy of Sciences and from Warsaw University spoke of the difficulty they encountered when attempting to publish their work in the West. Under martial law regulations, it was illegal for such works to be sent through the mail, so everything had to be done through an intermediary—perhaps someone leaving the country, perhaps an airline pilot.

It was widely discussed and accepted that 15 people associated in a professional capacity with Warsaw University were actually interned in early March of 1982, and, though the number was well under original Western estimates, the arrests created an unspoken threat that loomed over the scholars who either were or could be suspected of being politically active in the underground. The insidious influence of martial law dominated the university atmosphere, and the future of empirical research seemed to be at stake.

On March 2, 1982, I wrote in my diary:

> Talk at the university suggests that the secret police have many informants planted in the universities and work places. People surmise that, with a substantial decrease in the standard of living, the payoffs for secretly informing are considerable. Students, assistants and professors could go about their business and simultaneously keep notes on the conversations and activities of colleagues. A professor teaching a sociology course on the mechanisms of conformity has become more careful about the examples he uses than he was before martial law.
>
> The list of courses now offered in the Institute of Sociology shows that professors have not abandoned their subject matter, though the content of some of the courses has changed.
>
> Nevertheless, courses currently offered show courage on the part of the professors. Courses include:
> "Individuals and Society: Mechanisms of Conformity"

> "Interests and Values of Social Groups in the Polish In-
> stitutional System"
> "Contemporary Problems in Poland"
> Class discussions are often explicitly about the current
> martial law situation. Though certain radical professors
> continue to carry on, delivering rousing lectures, the sit-
> uation has precarious moments. *Milicja* [police] occupy
> seemingly permanent posts in many places in and around
> the university. They occasionally stop people and ask for
> documents. . . . My advisor told me that she believes so-
> ciologists will again be able to carry out their question-
> naire and fieldwork studies "someday, but we just don't
> know when."

My Polish "mama" confided to me strategies for
coping with the outward manifestations of martial
law—curfews, bugged telephones and identification
checks. But when it came to unspoken nuances of
behavior, guidance was more difficult. Poles themselves offered conflicting advice: "Even *we* don't know
how to behave in this situation," they said.

A Western friend wrote in her diary:

> Nothing is certain here. Today you can buy mineral
> water; tomorrow you can't. Today the censorship com-
> mittee lets you rehearse your play, but tomorrow it will
> decide not to let you perform it. Today the government
> refuses to bargain with Solidarity; tomorrow it agrees to.
> Today the passport office says I need *this* particular form
> to leave the country; the next day it is the wrong form. It
> is an odd feeling to be living in a country where there is
> no final word; no one knows for sure what is going on.

The atmosphere during those days was reflected
simply and starkly by a man selling apples in the
street. With tears in his eyes he pleaded to a pas-
serby, "What will become of us?"

1

Private
and Public Worlds

A Communist Party member serving as a government adviser invited me to march with him in the government-sponsored May Day parade. When I met him several weeks later, he told me proudly that his daughter participated in the Solidarity May Day demonstration. Later, I learned that he secured the release of several of his friends, arrested on suspicion of having engaged in planning the illegal May Day demonstration.

An employee took a desk from a state-owned factory, intending to resell it. He left the desk in a truck near his apartment building until it could be delivered to the intended purchasers. But to his dismay, it disappeared. He complained bitterly to his neighbors that "people are dishonest and immoral."

Two policemen harrassed me and blocked me from entering the American Embassy. Later that day, I ran into them, at the cosmetic counter of a shopping center. This time, they asked me to help pick out perfume for their girlfriends.

Poles lead two lives, the public and the private. Stories that reach the West tend to extoll Solidarity's virtues and present contemporary Poles as saints, who, in the face of incredible odds and at great personal risk, have become radical Solidarity activists. Poles tend to talk about things they think foreigners respect and omit more dubious parts foreigners may approve less of—even if they are the bane of Polish existence. Thus, Western writers did not usually learn how the Poles they interviewed obtained high-fashion French shoes or Italian boots— when the rationing system allowed each citizen one pair of Polish-made shoes per year (1982 and 1983).

In order to get by under trying economic and political conditions, Poles shape their selves to mesh with the varying demands of private and public worlds. They have developed a keen ability, not only to live with the contradictions of their society, but also to manipulate them creatively. At one and the same time, they are pulled by the cacophonous demands of individual and family needs on the one hand, and on the other hand, contemporary realities: a rigid bureaucracy, uneven market distribution, the constraints of official titles.

Poles participate in the standard rituals of public life but—literally, in order to survive in Polish society—they must continually show different sides of themselves. One moral code is reserved for the private world of family and friends, another one for the public. The Communist Party member who serves as a government advisor in the public eye, also acts as an advocate for Solidarity activists in trouble. The employee who himself "organizes" a desk, is indignant when someone "steals" the same desk from him. The policemen who try to prevent Poles from making contact with the embassy of an enemy country, go out of their way to make pleasant conversation with a citizen of that country.

Getting by in public life often calls for circumventing the system. A religious American couple working for a church relief distribution agency in Poland was stopped by police for speeding. The husband had neither a Polish nor an international driver's license. He lied to the policeman, claiming he had applied for the international license and it was delayed in the mail. The wife came to me, disturbed about their "moral decline": "We find ourselves lying more and more."

Indeed, when I looked back at the events of the past week, I realized that I, too, had almost automatically lied on several occasions. On Monday I had fabricated a story in order to get tickets for a concert that was sold out: "I am the wife of Robert Byrd from the American Embassy." On Tuesday I had weasled my way into getting an International Student ID card, not officially available to researchers or doctoral candidates. I bypassed some bureaucracy and claimed to be a student; the lie saved me several hundred dollars. On Wednesday I overslept, but I told the official I was to meet with that morning that the bus I was riding had broken down. Dishonesty had become so ingrained in my approach to bureaucracy and formal relations that when I returned to the United States several friends complained that I lied too much.

A lawyer summed up the Polish predicament: "Everything is so impossible that we have to avoid the law. We have to be more intelligent." The profound disregard for the legal system is expressed in the Polish proverb: "Laws exist only to be tested." Some situations demand dishonesty with authorities; others demand a mixture of truth and fiction. One does not always lie blatantly or tell the uncomfortable truth. Poles have learned to mix the two into credible stories to resolve bureaucratic problems or to talk their way out of trouble.

Respect for authority and reluctance to cheat are seen as naive. But lying is an art. One day as I rode the express bus, I noticed a large woman staring intently at me. Checks on buses and trams to make sure that people have bought tickets and punched them in a machine are rare, but this woman turned out to be a controller. Though I had with me a bus pass issued from the university, it was invalid for express buses. With righteous indignation not often seen in Polish officials of such rank, she nudged me and inquired: "You ride the express bus with a bus pass?" I pretended not to understand or speak Polish, and replied in English—"I don't understand."

A young woman standing next to me who spoke a little English began to translate, explaining that the pass is not good for the express bus. I said I hadn't realized that. Through the translator, the controller asked how long I had been in Poland. I said "for two months." But the controller noted that there were monthly stamps piled up for more than a year and a half on my pass. One sympathetic woman onlooker said, "Maybe she collects these stamps as souvenirs." Though I pretended not to understand what the onlooker had said, I chimed in English that "I collect them from all of my friends."

Everyone was on my side—the self-proclaimed translator who repeatedly told the controller, "But she didn't know;" a plump middle-aged man who reiterated, "But she's a foreigner;" and the woman who had suggested that "She collects the stamps as souvenirs." Even though the onlookers had probably caught on that I was lying, they had nothing but contempt for the controller and rooted for me during this public discussion of whether or not I should have to pay.

As soon as the bus stopped and the doors opened all other passengers without legitimate tickets scurried away, leaving me to the controller. She motioned for me to get off, and my recently acquired chorus of cheerleaders got off as well, though this was a remote bus stop. Since I was in a hurry and it was becoming clear that I would not escape paying the fine, I handed the controller the 600 złoty, and thanked the young woman for translating.

I later discovered I had not merely played the na-

ive foreigner by pretending I didn't understand Polish—I had been the naive foreigner. Friends told me
that, instead of paying the fine, I should have let the
controller write down my identification information
and address. "They'll send the bill in one month;
when you don't pay it they'll send you another bill
the second month. Only a year later they'll call you
into court. Since you're leaving in a month, you'll
never have to pay it. You honest American, your
mistake was to think you have to pay it. No Pole
ever pays such a fine on the spot. You wasted your
money."

They reasoned: "Though it is possible to skirt almost every rule, and to arrange almost everything
informally in this country, almost nothing is certain."

Though being a foreigner did not improve my
standing with the bus controller, the identity is often
helpful. Being a foreigner usually makes it easy to
meet people, but it generally limits these contacts to
public "performance" situations. Answers to questions in formal interviews are often predictable and
tailored to fit the interviewer. Officials have a vested
interest in presenting the economic and political situation in a certain light—at least in their offices. Less
official individuals are more apt to champion Solidarity and recite the injustices of martial law. But
neither officials nor others will tell you how they can
buy jackets for 30,000 złoty or sheep-skinned coats
for 200,000 złoty when their monthly income is
13,500 złoty (the average income in 1984). Such information is simply not the way most Poles present
themselves to foreigners.

It is also nearly impossible to determine people's
political affiliations and connections, which may be
quite different from what their statements suggest,
since many Poles sympathize with Solidarity in the
company of Westerners. They articulate their opinions to fit those of the listeners.

Can a foreigner get past public presentations? I addressed this issue during a public lecture I gave at Warsaw University. I had been asked to discuss my research in Poland, and I began the lecture by posing a serious question: "Is it possible for foreign observers to learn much about Poland?" Members of the audience, who usually nodded through lectures, sat up in their chairs, their curiosity piqued. There are a number of reasons why it is difficult for foreign observers to learn about Poland, I continued. The position of Westerners in Poland determines the prism through which they see events. Whatever the research method, the mere presence of a foreign researcher will influence the observed facts.

A professor in the audience volunteered a story about three Polish sisters. "There was a family in which there were three daughters. The eldest daughter married an engineer; the second married a teacher; and the third married a Frenchman." The speaker was entertaining the audience, but he underscored my point: the most important identity the Frenchman had was that of foreigner.

The audience was puzzled. I began my talk by addressing how Poles had been relating to me for the last two years and what lay behind it. I considered this question integral to my formal topic; my position as a foreigner unavoidably influenced my perspective on various spheres of activity in Poland.

To understand Polish political life, for instance, I had to investigate the role word of mouth information—gossip and rumor—plays in politics. To understand the economic situation, I had to investigate not only the official channels, but also the informal exchange of goods and services that is built on face-to-face contacts. To describe the network of interpersonal relationships, it was imperative that I understand who I was in the eyes of the people I knew and how my status as a foreigner—and my very presence—influenced how people behaved toward me. Only by placing my observations in the context of my foreign status could I know why I was likely to see certain things and unlikely to see others.

Similarly, if I wanted to learn about political attitudes, public opinion or the "political crises" which have received widespread media coverage in recent years, I had to have a feel for the aims various factions had in talking with me. For, without access to parts of people's private worlds, I would have to settle for official views and publicly approved explanations. In short, my understanding of Poland would be severely limited.

In Poland, Westerners are creatures from another world. They are unable to understand the Polish situation, no matter how much people might try to teach them. This is the reason Poles try to "take care" of foreigners; they may be criticized, but not in their presence. One university professor told me: "We do not criticize visiting scholars after their presentations because we do not consider it worthwhile. Westerners have deep-seated preconceptions, and they tend to consider themselves much better informed than we, the poor autochthons." During my three-year affiliation with the Institute of Sociology at Warsaw University, I observed "the ritual of listening to foreign guests."

When visiting scholars deliver lectures about research in Poland and the subject matter is uninteresting or misconceived, the Polish audience nevertheless sits attentively, feigning interest. The rules of the ritual dictate that the speaker may not be challenged, criticized or even questioned in any meaningful way. But it is clear to everyone, except the foreigner, that people are uncomfortable with what is being said. Listeners are privately disturbed, exchanging knowing glances with one another. The researcher, usually visiting for several days, weeks or months, goes home very satisfied. But his misconceptions and misinformation have been confirmed, not challenged. In brief interactions such as those carried on with visiting scholars or speakers, many Poles tend to insulate—even patronize—foreigners. Such interaction often deepens miscommunication and reinforces role-playing on both sides.

Behind the gestures of hospitality, helpfulness, politeness and a tendency to praise rather than criticize visitors is an understanding on the part of Poles that it is necessary to explain the basics to outsiders who have no point of reference for understanding the Polish world and the way it works. To emphasize the difference in perspective and experience, one friend even addressed me affectionately as "foreigner" instead of by name.

Often I would ask why, as in "Why doesn't this office supply store have paper?" or "Why can't I buy bus tickets in the provinces one day in advance?" My friend would smile and reply, "Why is not a Polish question." In the eyes of Polish hosts, the question "why" underscores foreigners' naivete and inability to understand how things really are. It underlines the difficulty of attaining private access.

Whether admired for their prosperity or humored for their naivete, foreigners are outsiders. Poles often laugh at the gullibility of foreigners behind their backs or simply joke affectionately with them, as one might poke fun at children.

While being a foreigner is constraining in that it insulates one from the private side of Polish life, the status is also illuminating. A foreigner is able to glide through a variety of *środowiska*, (social circles of potential friends, acquaintances or colleagues brought together by occupation or common experience). He easily avoids questions of social standing Poles encounter when they try to move from one group to another. He can be on *ty* or familiar terms with a much larger variety of Poles than can Poles themselves. In moving within and among most groups, the foreigner is above all, uninvolved; he is from another world. Being an outsider makes it possible to meet a variety of people, though usually in public "performance" situations.

Though there was a good deal of official anti-American sentiment at the time of my visit, my identity as American enabled me to glide through various social circles, including high government circles.

I was able to use my status as a Westerner to gain the help of Professor Pilichowski, high-ranking official in the Polish Justice Department's Central Commission for the Investigation of Nazi Crimes. The commission controlled access to Polish archives housing documents from World War II concentration camps. I wanted the documents for a research project. At a time when Polish reporters were consistently denied access to commission members, I easily arranged a meeting with Professor Pilichowski. Polish friends coached me on what to wear—a black velvet jacket and skirt, frilly white blouse and black high-heeled shoes—and on how to act. A friend had read in the newspaper that General Jaruzelski would send Professor Pilichowski flowers that week in celebration of his 70th birthday. At the friend's suggestion, I arrived with a bouquet of carnations in honor of the same occasion—seven flowers, one for each decade. The professor received me enthusiastically and warmly; he considered my project worthwhile and interesting for Poles as well as for Americans. Our meeting was a typically Polish mixture of business and personal matters. The professor sent his secretaries scurrying to find documents necessary for my research, while he chatted about family matters and thanked me again and again for the flowers. I left with assured access to the archives and Professor Pilichowski's personal support. The official media was strongly anti-American after President Reagan imposed economic sanctions against

Poland, yet I was treated with royal hospitality by
Polish government officials.

An outsider has difficulty penetrating a Pole's public
face to understand the layers of a more private world.
But that separation of public and private worlds is
one which guides the Polish people's actions towards
each other as well.

The "public versus private" nature of Polish life
can be observed everywhere. Poles live a dual world
every day. It is the discrepancy between ration card
allocations of meat and the amounts found on private tables; the difference between what people read
in the official press and what they believe and repeat
to each other as truth; the contrast between the lackadaisical unconcern for state work and the tireless
industry devoted to unofficial jobs. It is the gap between what people do and what they say.

Behavior reserved for private life would be completely out of place in public life. In private life Poles
are warm and give freely of their time; in public life
they are often rude and have no time. In private life
conversation is friendly and relaxed; in public life
speech is guarded and formal. In private, over vodka
and herring, people talk about life with a shared in-
tensity.

The setting and atmosphere of public life is imper-
sonal, ritualized and standardized. A friend who returned to Poland after living abroad for several years
related his first impressions: "No one wants to do
anything in this country. While waiting in line people slouch with their legs crossed, arms on hips. From
time to time they sigh and change posture. Mothers
discipline explorative children who have not yet lost
their curiosity. Without expression or emotion, people stare into space."

Stoicism covers deep, underlying anger. In daily
public life, cold competitiveness occasionally surfaces when people argue while waiting in line, or

push and shove in crowded buses and trams. The son of an army officer described the atmosphere:

> A person is a wolf in relation to another—he regards everyone as his enemy. From the point of view of social order, it is good that people restrain themselves. But from the point of view of human psychology, it is not good because it creates stress, frustration—and that eats at the organism. A few individuals who can't manage to control themselves are aggressive towards you. For example, if I were with you in a crowded tram and people pushed me, you would kick me in the feet, and I would be even more angry. And I would say something very unkind. Notice how people behave in trams, that is an atmosphere in which one feels such discontent, such rigidity. Those people are not normal—among us everyone is odd. There are very few people who act as they really are. The rest wear masks. They pretend to be what they aren't because the whole situation—this deceptiveness and mutual hostility—makes them that way.

When pent-up anger surfaces, it can be explosive. As customers quibbled about their respective places in a long line for mineral water, a pale-faced clerk, weary from a day's work, threw a bottle to the cement floor. As it crashed she pleaded, "Stop it. One goes crazy listening to this bickering from morning till evening."

Privacy has no place in routine and common public life. A West German woman living in Poland was shocked by her visit to a public gynecological clinic. A nurse was sitting in the waiting room for women only. As the women walked in, the nurse filled out a form for each one, demanding answers to a series of gynecological questions. Everyone in the waiting room could hear the questions and responses. The West German was even more startled, however, to see that the door to the examination room was open. Nurses walked in and out of the room, chatting about the latest films and the delivery of fish to a nearby store. Remembering how Polish women tended to speak of gynecological matters with discretion, I asked a friend how such lack of privacy was possible. Her answer was simple. "The clinic is a public place."

In striking contrast to public life, the atmosphere of private life is emotional, personal and intimate. Private life reduces, if only momentarily, the individual's feelings of personal anxiety. *Swój człowiek* (one of us) is someone who thinks like you, someone you have accepted into your confidence. *Swój człowiek*, someone you understand because the two of you share a set of beliefs and values, enjoys the sympathy and compassion of the community. Those who are, for each other, *swój człowiek* form an exclusive group. The standardized, formal way of responding to a foreigner is definitely for someone who is not *swój człowiek*. It is impossible to be viewed as a foreigner and to be considered *swój człowiek* at the same time. This does not mean, however, that a foreigner can never come to be *swój człowiek* with some people at some moments. But, at the moment he is *swój człowiek*, he no longer has the identity of a foreigner.

In Poland, those who are *swój człowiek* to each other engage in intimate, intense and usually frequent interaction. They often drink, play bridge or take vacations together. They take on the business of each other's lives. Within the small circle of family and friends, close sharing and considerable involvement in one another's lives is considered appropriate.

With friends it is necessary to eat, drink, and bare one's soul; then to eat, drink and pour out one's soul some more. No event is social without food and drink, and people will offer both no matter how little they may have. Poles invite others into their homes for feasts, drinking, and heartfelt emotional conversation. It is a matter of honor to be committed and truthful to friends.

A Polish friend was puzzled by a letter from his old girlfriend, now a student at Harvard. "How can it be that every week she can meet twenty new people but still feel lonely?" he wanted to know. In Poland, people have fewer friends but are committed to the friends they have.

Drinking is a main form of socializing in Poland. Almost every adult social gathering features a table decked with vodka and *zakąska* (the food that accompanies vodka). Vodka is central to Polish life; weddings, reunions, namesday celebrations at home and at work, and "parties" in which friends gather round the kitchen table require ample supplies of the drink. At vodka celebrations, people propose toasts and coax each other to drink, often for hours at a time. Drinking vodka together signifies intimacy and recognition as *swój człowiek*. When the bounds of the inner circle are in doubt, characterizing the person in question as *swój człowiek* indicates he has been accepted. When a Pole hesitated to talk openly with a person he had just met, his friends assured him, "You can talk politics with him. He is *swój człowiek*."

People of the same *środowisko* (social circle) participate in celebrations with vodka. Company can be mixed as long as people belong to the same social circle, though often men drink with men and women with women.

Celebrations at which vodka is consumed are a crucial component of social life, and participation in them creates a spirit of belonging and community. This community spirit demands validation, and it is considered an unsociable and ungracious gesture not to down a shot of vodka when a toast has been proposed.

Urbanites will coax a visitor to drink a little, to drink vodka, to down vodka, to get drunk, to toast, to toast some more. . . . But, if one really does not want to participate, there are ways of saying no. Among peasants, however, the rules are much stricter. Accepting drink is a matter of morality. One must drink with friends to be considered morally right.

An urban friend, Edmund, once attended a party in the village in which his summer home was located. Everyone was completely drunk, and by two in the morning Edmund felt he had had enough to drink. He noticed that an elderly man was preparing to leave. Edmund offered to walk the man home, thinking it an acceptable excuse for leaving. The elderly man was so happy, so grateful and appreciative of the escort that he invited Edmund inside and, to my friend's dismay, produced a jug of *bimber* (home brew). Edmund at first declined but eventually gave in to the pressure of rural hospitality. The two of them toasted until the entire bottle had been consumed; refusal would have affronted morality and personal honor. Edmund was sick for two days.

Drinking is an essential social ritual. The phrase "I never drank vodka with him" indicates that he has not been accepted into the inner circle. Drinking parties reflect the Polish public-private split. Though people become uninhibited with alcohol, a celebration with vodka is nevertheless a ritualized formal occasion with strict rules. People lose control in a controlled way. They are expected to reveal the profound issues in their lives. But those who become unacceptably unrestrained, violating the rules of the ritual, are criticized with: "He doesn't know how to drink." Poles do not fool around when they drink socially; they philosophize.

A Polish scholar visiting the United States told me he could not understand the source of amusement or purpose in American parties. "People act in the same way at parties as they do in everyday life," he said. "No one says or does anything he doesn't say or do otherwise." The scholar was accustomed to the intimate atmosphere and community spirit of Polish parties.

In some social circles participation in vodka celebration is a prerequisite for making a career. Vodka, for instance, is a fundamental part of the lives of many

Communist Party apparatchiks and politicians who are or must become "our man" for success. Vodka facilitates the transition from an official to an unofficial situation. This allows wangling which could not be done officially. Vodka promotes the privatization of public roles. Those who want to make careers in the Party must drink vodka and participate in "drinking-bouts" within their Party circle. A celebration with vodka often turns into an intimate emotional and intellectual affair, as well as an acceptable psychological release for people caught up in ambivalence over conflicting public and private lives.

Polish formality and reserve arise partially from an instinct to survive in a climate of fear and uncertainty. In the marketplace and on the street corner people often speak in euphemisms. That way, they can convey some private information in public. Euphemisms need not always be obscure or unintelligible to others. Though the underlying meaning may be obvious to most, the euphemism is still used to maintain appearances.

I once watched in disbelief as a woman illegally changed dollars at the black market price over a tapped telephone. She asked her friend who deals in the buying and selling of dollars, "Would you like some green material? There's lots of this green material, you could sew a dress with it." Obviously, the woman was trying to sell dollars, not fabric.

Poles are masters of poise in conveyance of nuance through language, even among friends in private life. The subtleties of language serve to mask private intentions when distinctions between public and private are complex and sometimes confused.

The boyfriend of a French woman living in Poland was interned by police for political activities in the early months of martial law. They were to have had dinner together on the day he was imprisoned. Several days later, the woman received a letter from him smuggled out of prison. It began like this:

(name of prison, date)

Dear Natalie,

First of all I must apologize for my absence at Sunday's dinner. I am very sorry indeed I couldn't see you on that day. Now everything is clear: I am interned and the only thing to do is wait.

The first sentence of the letter sounds like a serious apology from one who stood up his lover. The boyfriend thereby displayed his pride by pretending to ignore his own situation. The letter illustrates a potent, distilled way of communicating: few words convey a lot of meaning.

Likewise, an acquaintance of mine received a Polish passport and a tourist visa to vacation in West Germany for two weeks. She left letters for friends and instructed them to open the letters if she had not returned to Poland in two weeks. One letter thanked a colleague for lending useful books and for her help and friendship and wished her good luck in her career. The letter said nothing overt about emigrating, but it was clear to the colleague that the woman would not come back to Poland after her "vacation."

The formalities of public life and the language people use maintain a mantle of normalcy that enshrouds informal dealings and private life. Public displays mask the informal organization behind them, for to reveal it would challenge the entire public facade. People have an enormous stake in preserving a public persona: it is in almost no one's interest to unmask "public life." Consummate survivors, Poles have learned how to say one thing, do another, and not go mad in the living of this ambiguity. In its ritual character, public life provides a stark contrast to what people do unofficially. Yet it is the ritual aspects themselves which enable people to deal with the contradictions.

The Solidarity movement can be understood as an attempt to escape from the tension and weariness bred by the ritualization of public life. Solidarity was called a "revolution of common sense." In content and even, to some extent, in form, it was a response to and an attack upon this ritualization.

Life in Poland demands living on two levels. Knowledge of accepted yet contradictory conventions is the key to getting along. Poles cannot afford to be lackadaisical if they are to survive amid scarcity and turmoil. They must take certain risks, yet undertake relationships and carry out their strategies alertly, with sensitivity and subtlety. Both the rituals of public life and the transactions of private life are requisite for survival.

People organize their lives within a public-private dichotomy. It is imprinted in Polish minds, yet Poles are ambivalent about having to operate within such circumstances. This dual system has a long history and present day Poles have had a lifetime to adjust to its confusing demands; but while they pride themselves on successful private deals, many are ashamed of employing this route to success. It is, however, the system's very flexibility—and the satisfaction people feel when they are able to manipulate it informally and privately—that sustains the Polish people as they face ongoing hardship.

As an outsider, I was able to untangle *some* of the complexities of the Polish public and private demeanor. After more than two years of living in Poland, I asked a friend, "Am I *swój człowiek?*"

"Sometimes," he replied.

2

"This Is Everyday Life for Us"

Several weeks after arriving in Poland in February, 1982, I held a party in my apartment for a number of Polish friends. An 11:00 martial law curfew had been imposed, and police patrols were stationed in strategic and often unlikely locations around Warsaw, checking personal identification cards—required of all citizens at all times—and stopping both pedestrians and automobiles. The party would break up early due to the curfew, though under normal circumstances in Poland the high spirits would have lasted long into the early morning.

Private social gatherings provide relief and release from the sobriety of public life. My guests arrived shortly before 7:00, each bearing one small bottle of precious vodka, purchased with a ration card. (In the beginning of martial law, only one such card per month was allotted under the government rationing system.) By 9:00 everyone had scurried for wraps to bundle themselves against the frigid winter, concerned about whether the often unreliable public transportation would deliver them to distant apartment buildings before "police hour," as the curfew was called.

During our brief two hours together, intense discussion focused on our fears, heightened as they were by martial law. In the closed-off country, with little hint of the outside world, the atmosphere of martial law loomed oppressively. Grażyna, a strikingly attractive physician in her late twenties, described the arrest of her brother's friend. She also wondered if her boyfriend, earning hard currency in West Germany, would actually return to Poland; she had heard nothing from him since the imposition of martial law. Janusz, a 32-year-old engineer with a wide smile, spoke of "militarization" at the government plant where he worked. Ala, a 30-year-old photographer, worried that her plans to visit her sister in London and exhibit her work there might not be realized.

Spotting some American popular magazines lying around my apartment, several guests politely asked permission to look at them. The magazines became a diversion from the main topic of discussion—politics. Eagerly leafing through the glossy pages, my friends squealed over sleek late-model cars, chic fashions, juicy gossip columns and movie star prattle. Pronouncing judgement on American preoccupation with psychoanalysis, Janusz observed, "In Poland no one has time for therapy, since we spend all of our time shopping. But since Americans spend only five minutes in a supermarket, they have to go to psychiatrists because they're bored."

We toasted one another with rye vodka until Grażyna began to read to us an article entitled "The Good News About Moods" in the February, 1982, *Cosmopolitan*. The author described how people should go about solving their problems and feeling better. Grażyna launched into a lively parody, informing us how to endure the trials and tribulations of the everyday. Flamboyantly, she recited an impromptu translation of the following paragraph:

> Let's suppose the brand new space heater you bought last fall breaks down in the below-zero cold snap, and the dealer shrugs off your complaint, maintaining that he's not responsible for repairs. Spare your clocks, your china, your friends—and don't let your rage retreat into a head-

ache. This is the time, as they say in Brooklyn, to open your mouth. Call that dealer back and let him know you don't like being shafted. Demand a new machine—delivered to your door. If he remains intractable, put your complaint in writing to the Better Business Bureau and send copies to his competitors. If you charged the machine, call the credit card company and ask for their help in making restitution.

We laughed. To find, much less pay for, a brand-new space heater in Warsaw was nearly impossible. For my friends, such ways of solving problems were but American absurdities: to have a working telephone; to actually get through to the dealer; to find him at all responsive.

My guests found the notion that any dealer would try to rectify a problem preposterous. That he would come up with a new machine was dismissed as ludicrous and that he would deliver it to the door, inconceivable. Again, we laughed. The existence of a Better Business Bureau seemed far-fetched. And that a consumer could send copies of the letter to the dealer's competitors seemed absurd, since there are no competitors—retail networks in Poland are monopolies. As for credit cards, my friends considered them nonsensical plastic objects from another world.

Simply, the thought of using such problem-solving techniques and the idea that they might be successful in Poland were inconceivable to them. In Poland, strategies for seeking restitution are grounded not in formal procedures but in social networks, which circumvent such procedures.

When I mention to American friends that I have researched the Polish informal economy, the first response I hear is, "Oh, you mean you studied the black market." Actually, there is much more involved. Informal exchange is based on a complex network of social relationships and elaborate etiquette. "Black market" carries connotations of shady, yet direct transactions. Exchange within the Polish informal economy, however, is respectable; it takes time and involves long-term commitments.

In the absence of Western-style business relationships, Poles use social networks to solve their everyday problems and to accomplish day-to-day tasks ranging from buying batteries to resolving bureaucratic impasses to bailing out arrested friends or family members. Private arrangements and exchanges—sometimes between private persons, sometimes reaching into official circles—are the very threads that hold together the tapestry of Polish life.

Contrary to the Western perception that no one in Poland can get anything, almost everyone can get something. Almost everyone has a commodity or benefit to exchange or sell, be it a relief package from abroad, a desk stolen from a workplace or access to the state bureaucracy in charge of apartment allocation.

The informal economy is made up of private activities, both legal and illegal, that are conducted in conjunction with the exchange of commodities, such as goods, services, benefits, privileges and information. Privately arranged exchanges involve commodities and activities technically either legal or illegal. I may illegally procure a good for you, and you may return the favor in 10 years by helping to prepare my daughter's wedding reception. In order to make a successful informal arrangement, parties to the transaction must establish a "private" relationship, even if the transaction takes place in a formal context in which one or more parties are officially in their "public" roles. Private arrangements, both legal and illegal, are an integral part of and firmly rooted in practically every area of Polish economic and social life—from private exchanges to the state bureaucracy to legal, institutionalized private enterprises, cooperatives and services.

It is impossible to measure the extent of the informal economy, but, even by official accounts, informal economic activities are substantial and endemic. In a 1984 article in the official newspaper, *Życie Gospodarcze (Economic Life)*, Marek Bednarski, an economist, defines the informal economy as "any economic activity that is not directly registered by state statistical services because of existing accounting methods, the inefficiency of the data collecting system or inability to obtain information; consequently, such activity is not centrally controlled or regulated." Bednarski goes on to estimate that Poles spend 20–30 percent of their income on goods and services not registered by taxation authorities, that is, illegally produced goods and services.

I asked one of Poland's foremost sociologists why the living economy—the informal one—has received so little attention from social scientists. His answer was simple: "This is just everyday life for us." For almost everyone in Poland, even the intellectual elite, private arrangements are a way of life. My introduction to Poland was an education in the ways of informal give and take—in the ways of a society which is extremely sophisticated in terms of individual need and help.

THE ETIQUETTE OF *ZAŁATWIĆ*

In February of 1982 I wrote in my journal:

Three of my acquaintances—Polish women whose husbands are in the West—are unable to obtain passports to leave the country, though they had had passports in their possession before martial law was imposed two months ago. I spent several hours with one of those women today. She is desperate—goes from office to office. Each office tells her to go to the next, to go back to the former office, to obtain a new document. When she produces the document, she is told she needs yet another.

Private arrangements provide a way through the maze of Polish bureaucracy. One afternoon, not long after talking to the woman, I looked on in disbelief as a prominent writer telephoned the passport office after having downed half a bottle of vodka. "My name is Włodek," he said to the woman who answered. "I'm not good looking, but I'm very intelligent. Are we going to get down to basics and talk to each other as *ty*?" He proceeded to explain that she had "a mess in her office." The application he had filled out for a passport to Norway had been lost again. He was scheduled to leave Poland in one week and still had not received a passport. The woman replied that she could not solve the problem entirely over the phone but invited him to arrive at the office at a certain hour and come directly to her instead of waiting in line. Two days later, he had a passport in hand. Though a drunken telephone conversation is not the usual means of establishing a private relationship, the tactic worked.

I came to realize how critical networks and contacts were to accomplishing my goals. My position as a foreign researcher provided me with extensive contacts; scholars and institute scientists offered me generous help. Had the average Pole arrived without introduction at a Polish research institute or government office, he would have had little or no access to materials. Because respected academics and public officials took a personal interest in me as a foreigner, however, almost anything could be arranged. Employees went to great lengths to produce desired information. Personal contacts, facilitated by my status as a Westerner, were central to my success as a researcher. I used such connections as a Pole might, but scholars I was in touch with assisted me without ulterior motive. They went out of their way.

One sociologist who was particularly friendly and helpful invited me to her apartment. Pani Professor

M. eagerly greeted me at the door of her cozy apartment. Inside, spotless white paint contrasted with rich handcrafted wooden cabinets, a world far different from the dark, cold elevator, cement apartment entrance and hallways. A plump lady, my hostess was dressed in a revealingly low cut, bright red dress, a white handmade shawl and black high-heeled shoes. Her brown hair was styled on top of her head, and it appeared she had just come from the hairdresser; her dramatic make-up was thickly applied, her nails brightly polished. The outfit would have been totally inappropriate for an academic making a professional contact in the United States. In Poland, however, every successful business arrangement is based on a private relationship; Pani Professor M., a well-respected scholar, was accordingly "dressed for success."

She asked what I was researching and how she could be of help. She coaxed me to partake of cakes, coffee and strawberries her husband had picked from their small garden plot in the countryside. Was I of Polish descent? What state in America was I from? Her daughter, an engineer, worked in Washington, D.C., and I gathered from the tone of Pani Professor M.'s voice that the daughter did not plan to return to Poland.

Pani Professor M.'s help was invaluable to my research. Since her books were difficult to get in bookstores—only a set number is printed, regardless of demand—she loaned me precious copies of some of them and gave me others.

Pani Professor M. also wrote letters of introduction for me to sociologists and arranged contact with the directors of several government institutes. Her close friend, a director at the government's Central Statistical Office, would help me get all the statistical information I wanted once he returned from his extended vacation in Denmark. "If you go on your own without making an appointment, the people there will tell you, 'We don't have those statistics,' " she told me.

Indeed, the division director greeted me cordially after Pani Professor M.'s introduction, gave me as much information as he could and referred me to persons in other divisions of the Central Statistical Office who gave me the rest of the material I wanted. Without Pani Professor M.'s personal interest in my affairs, I would have found gathering statistical data much less pleasant; I appreciated her generous help very much.

On another occasion a friend arranged for me to meet a former cabinet member, currently a professor doing research in my field. In keeping with the personal approach to what Americans would consider strictly business matters, male scholars often introduced me to colleagues with compliments about my appearance. When I arrived at the university office of the former government official, he kissed my hand and said that I was "a charming lady." With bright eyes, he said I looked like a living Mona Lisa and inquired if I had seen the original in Paris. He took my coat, apologizing that there was not a coat hanger in the room, and added, "In Poland the conditions aren't too good." He summoned his secretary to get us tea, apologizing profusely because he had no coffee to offer, and handed me a homegrown pear. The professor asked, as had many people, if I was related to the famous family which founded the Polish chocolate factory "Wedel," known all over Europe before World II and later socialized by the postwar government. He boasted of relatives in the United States—he thought they lived in Buffalo.

Only after conversation about personal matters did we move on to professional ones. The professor talked about his research and provided me with several of his articles. He had written for both Church and Party publications.

Before I left, he asked for an address so he could send me a "New Year's greeting." As he helped me with my coat, he told me that "my future husband would have a pretty wife" and that "we would have pretty children."

By American standards the meeting might seem inappropriately personal, indeed, offensively so. But a personal tone characterized it precisely because the professor wanted me to feel welcome and to make our visit a pleasant one. In Poland, almost all successful business contacts are built on personal relationships which must be developed before business can transpire. The professor's conduct was appropriate and even accomplished. Had he eliminated the personal element he would have seemed cold and unhelpful by Polish standards.

Private arrangements are so prevalent in Polish life that an entire language has evolved in reference to them. This language is only roughly translatable. Specific terms embody key concepts—ways of thought and approach to life in Poland—that can only be conveyed in context. Many of them can be found in the diaries and memoirs of those who experienced the German occupation of Poland. Still others are connected with the post–World War II government and took on their present meaning and significance after the war. Terms for dealing in the informal economy are used often in everyday life.

Poles learn how to *załatwić sprawy* (to acquire goods or services provided by the formal structure, often using informal means). *Załatwić* is a verb translated "to arrange" or "to settle," but, in some contexts, it is better characterized as "to wangle" or "to finagle." *Załatwić* can refer to a broad variety of arrangements. *Sprawa* is a noun which means "a matter" or "an affair." Buying furniture, finding a babysitter, purchasing a coat, obtaining an apartment and being granted a job promotion can all be *"sprawy* to be *załatwione."*

The meaning of *załatwić* can best be understood by the founding of an all-purpose private agency not long ago in Warsaw. For a price, the agency will *załatwić* almost anything—from shopping or buying train tickets to caring for sick people or following the husbands of jealous wives. The bureau's advertisement reads: "We will help with every problem; we will *załatwić* every *sprawę*. Nothing is impossible for us." One of the duties the agency advertises is the "*załatwiania* of all *spraw* within the bureaucracy."

Conversation at a bus stop, in a taxi line or in a store provides ample evidence of widespread private arrangements. "I have a *sprawę* to *załatwić*" may refer to a seemingly simple matter—buying yogurt, making a telephone call or checking out a library book. But yogurt might not be available, the telephone out of order, the book checked out and obtainable only with the good graces of the librarian. Even these matters can become *sprawy* to *załatwienie*—that is, if straightforward channels are not productive, they may have to be arranged in a manner which circumvents institutionally approved ways of doing things. Though such matters need not necessarily be problematic, the idea that they may in fact become complicated is built into the meaning of *załatwić*.

People talk often of *sprawy* to be *załatwione*. There is even a term "to *załatwić* through the bar," which implies that a drinking partner will help *załatwić sprawę* solely because of the intimacy created by drinking together.

Such terms serve to mask the nature of the particular *sprawę* at hand to be finagled. They build in a purposeful ambiguity to the language and activities of everyday life in a society in which one's own *sprawy* are part of private rather than public life. "*Załatwić sprawę*," for example, can refer obliquely to almost any activity or matter. If I tell someone in conversation I have a *sprawę* to *załatwić* and must be on my way, I need not provide specifics. Though the *sprawa* might be completely trivial or legal, the point is that no one will know if this is the case or if, in fact, the *sprawa* is devious or illegal. *Sprawy* are rarely discussed with parties not directly involved. The general concept of a task to be accomplished or a matter outstanding is conveyed without divulging the nature of a particular *sprawa*.

Ambiguity in language and meaning is also accomplished through specific language patterns. Rather than hearing that one bought or received through bribery or as a present such things as fabric, a pair of shoes or an apartment, one hears instead, "I got an apartment." One simply "receives" things passively. Such language patterns make it unnecessary to explicate the active mechanism of acquisition.

Making private arrangements requires knowledge of the etiquette of *załatwić*. Parties to negotiation of private arrangements must enter into the negotiation according to certain unspoken rules and procedures. The expression *na lewo*, which translates literally as "on the left," means "outside of official channels" or, in idiomatic English, "under the table," or "through the back door." To live successfully *na lewo*, one must know how to make implicit and explicit agreements and how to perform the necessary rituals.

Agreements are entered into step-by-step, subtly and cautiously. I practiced some finer points of negotiation when I tried to obtain several pieces of leather luggage. In a small leather goods store in the Polish city of Cracow, I saw a beautiful tan leather briefcase. I was surprised to see it displayed in the store window rather than kept in the warehouse by employees and returned as soon as the store reopened.

The briefcase had disappeared from the shelf, so I described it to a clerk and asked if there were any left. He told me to return the next day at 10:00 A.M. to talk with the manager. The next morning yet another clerk informed me that the manager had gone to see the doctor and would be back in the afternoon. I returned later, found the manager in and inquired about the briefcase. As I had expected, the manager informed me the briefcase was already sold out. So I gently, but insistently expressed my desire to have such a briefcase: "That briefcase is very important to me," I said several times in a firm tone. "I can't tell you how important it is for me."

At length the manager looked straight at me and responded with facial expressions and a few whispered words. She took care to pay attention to the others in the store who continually fired questions at her. As soon as some people left, others drifted in, so I loitered here and there in the shop for 45 minutes, waiting to speak with the manager. Eventually, the shop cleared so we could talk. The manager said she knew what I wanted and could tell me more on Friday.

On Friday the manager again waited until the shop was almost empty, but this time she motioned me into the storeroom and showed me the briefcase. On display it had been priced at 2,500 złoty (in 1985 about $17.00 at the official exchange rate, or about $5.00 on the black market), yet the manager now quoted a price of 3,200 złoty. I gave her a 5,000 złoty bill, and the manager turned to get change. I objected profusely, "No, no. Please keep the change. I know you put yourself out, and I really appreciate your help. Thank you very much. . . ."

The manager asked several times, "Are you sure you don't want the change back?" I replied each time in the negative.

The manager thanked me in turn, then proceeded to show me all the good quality leather products in the storeroom, explaining that she could obtain more goods like these if I was interested. I described a suitcase bag I wanted to have and mentioned that I was leaving in a few days for a trip to the States.

The manager reminded me that it might be difficult to procure the bag in such a short time. "In order for our shop to be able to get things of quality," the manager explained, "I have to pay off people in the central warehouse." Then she added proudly, "I'm good at it. They know my store is number one, and they give me a lot of things."

I again thanked the manager for her generous efforts in obtaining the briefcase, and she commented on its beauty. "I would be very, very thankful and appreciative if you might be able to get the suitcase by Saturday. But, of course, I don't want to put you out. . . ."

On Saturday the manager produced the suitcase and insisted that I partake of tea and cherries. She quizzed me on my tastes in leather goods and promised to save me what I liked. Knowing I was travelling to the States, the manager politely and apologetically suggested a possible favor. "You know, my husband has low blood pressure, and it's hard to get coffee, let alone good coffee, without dollars in Poland." Knowing the manager would be offended had I offered money instead of a present at this point in our relationship, I picked up on the suggestion immediately. I told her I would be more than happy to bring her coffee when I returned. "I would be very appreciative," said the manager. I had been accepted into the manager's confidence.

The manager and I entered into the agreement step-by-step, with caution, subtlety and sensitivity. Negotiating private arrangements in Poland demands an understanding of the implicit rules of *załatwić*. Some trust between us had to exist before I could obtain the briefcase. By offering to procure more luggage and asking me to bring back coffee from the States, the manager showed me her door was open to future exchanges.

Success requires patience and tact. If I want to obtain a quality leather bag which the manager is keeping hidden for private exchanges, I cannot burst into the store and announce, "I'm sure you could use some coffee. How about that leather bag?" The manager would be offended and distrustful. By the same token, I must not take the answer "no" or "it's not available" at face value. To *załatwić* something demands persistence, discreet conduct and attention to the etiquette of exchange.

The manager and I did not engage in barter, but rather carried on a process of negotiation. We negotiated not only about leather goods, but more importantly, about our relationship. Neither I nor the manager could have initially predicted the outcome of our negotiations. The rituals of etiquette help to reduce ambivalence among negotiating parties.

Swój człowiek (one of us) is often used to refer to someone such as a civil servant or a store clerk with whom one has become acquainted and with whom one has consequently been able to make some kind of an agreement. A general feature of public life is that it is penetrated by private life, since one has to privatize a relationship in order to *załatwić*. The backstage sharing of vodka and sandwiches or, in the case of me and the manager, tea and cherries, is central to a successful arrangement. I now call the manager "Pani Jadzia," a diminutive form of Mrs. Jadwiga. The next step in the continuation of our relationship will be for me to "remember" "Pani Jadzia" on her name day and to bring her flowers or a present. From now on, I will be able to procure the luggage for the official price and tip the manager with an occasional present.

In other cases, if a scarce good or service is worth a lot of money, it is acceptable to give a tip of money. But money must be offered with the greatest of care. The party proposing it must emphasize that the money has nothing in common with a bribe: it is "gratuitous" or "unrenumerated." He must graciously thank the one he is offering money for the favor and underscore that the money is "nothing." He must repeat "please don't be offended" and stress that the proposed gift of money is unrelated to the fact that a *sprawa* has been or will be *załatwiona* for him.

Proposing money as "thanks" rather than as a bribe gives the person being offered it the opportunity to turn it down. It also protects the person offering it. As one friend put it: "Both parties can step back if necessary."

Pani R., an acquaintance of mine, is particularly adept at doing what Poles need to do to survive. She wheedles bureaucrats and manipulates her varied connections. Pani R. is a middle-level administrator in the Ministry of Health. When she needs to take a day off, she has a physician acquaintance sign a required paper stating that she is ill, so she can use the day to *załatwić sprawy*.

On one of her days off, Pani R. woke at dawn to leave for the market. She passed to the heads of lines for bread rolls and milk, since she knows the young women behind the counters. She did not recognize the homely clerk wearing a new dress at the cheese counter. Since the clerk was new, Pani R. had never made a deal with her. Though Pani R. got nothing special hidden behind the cheese counter that day, she earned the new clerk's good favor for the next time by telling her she looked "like a queen."

Keeping in mind that she had to arrange her son's wedding, she was constantly alert to prospective bargains. She had already obtained pork from relatives in a village, Hungarian wine from a private store and cooking oil from a neighbor who had received a relief package from West Germany. Hearing that a shipment of beef had just arrived, she rushed to the meat counter, where the clerks had already set aside some choice cuts for her. She asked if mineral water

had arrived yet, and the clerks repeated the rumor
that it would probably be there sometime in the
afternoon.

It was late morning by the time Pani R. rushed
home to make several important telephone calls, one
to a former colleague who she thought might be able
to help in arranging theater tickets for guests coming
to town.

Before she could get in the door, the laundry
woman appeared. She was officially working at the
state laundry, but had come to deliver a load of Pani
R.'s clean towels and sheets picked up the night before. She had laundered them at work and had taken
special care to keep them separate from the common
loads. Pani R. thanked her, giving her 1,500 złoty,
a generous sum for the laundry woman, who earns
11,000 złoty per month at her state job.

Then Pani R.'s sister-in-law called to say she was
concerned about her ailing 86-year-old father. The
heat in his building had been turned off and tem-
peratures outside were subfreezing. Did Pani R. know
of anyone from whom she could borrow or buy an
electric heater? Pani R. said she would think about
possibilities but, glancing at her watch, realized she
had to hurry.

She had an appointment with a private seamstress
for a clothes fitting. Arriving right before dinner—
the main meal of the day, eaten around two or three
in the afternoon—might irritate the woman, who
would soon begin preparing it for her husband. Pani
R.'s son had taken the family car, so she tried to
order a taxi by telephone since the nearby taxi stand
was likely to have a long line of people. She dialed
the number for fifteen minutes without getting
through. Hurriedly leaving her apartment, she waved
down an ambulance. It, too, was available for a price,
though private individuals almost always charge more
than professional taxi drivers.

Returning from the seamstress's, she saw a line in

front of a store. People leaving it were carrying rolls of coarse brown paper. She immediately ordered the cab driver to stop, and went to wait in line for, as it turned out, 45 minutes. While "waiting" in line, she made a telephone call to her sister-in-law, who came to join her. Each came home with ten rolls, the maximum amount one person could buy at a time. Pani R. gave five of her rolls to her son's family.

Private arrangements are time-consuming: it is necessary to go once to make contact; a second time to get what one wants; a third time with a present; and a fourth time again for something one wants.

The etiquette of exchange requires that one not be impatient. A woman who tried to *załatwić* a bureaucratic matter complained to the bureaucrat that she "didn't have time to wait in line." The bureaucrat was polite to others, but directed her to wait at the end of the line.

However, after such a day, Pani R. is less tired than I am after describing her.

As a friend joked, "Poland is truly a hunting and gathering society. If you see it, shoot it." Everybody shops all the time. People constantly look in store windows to see what can be had and ask those standing in line what they are waiting for.

I asked Pani R. how she felt about *spekulacja* (a private sale at greatly exaggerated prices of goods originally procured by the sellers from state stores or relief supplies). "There are various kinds of *spekulacja*. I'm generally for it because that's why I'm able to buy a lot of things," she told me. "That's the only way I was able to buy beef today."

Pani R. is not, by nature, an opportunist, but a warm person with a rare genuineness. She is hospitable, offering guests plenty of meat and vodka even in unplentiful times. Refusing to serve anything but the best, she coaxes visiting co-workers into drinking straight vodka just after breakfast. Punctuating her speech with big gestures and speaking as though a fire engine is hot on her tail, Pani R. amuses her guests. "In Poland there is joy," she says. "Today I have hot water, *and* the elevator is working."

Everyone loves Pani R.—everyone from her colleagues at work to the woman who sells newspapers, shampoo, stamps, toys and cigarettes in the newstand nearby. She makes even the laundry woman feel special. Her human and caring side comes across daily.

Pani R. has many facets—she is resourceful, inventive, clever and personable. And she masters the Polish system through versatility and skillful maneuvering.

Each working person has two roles, a private and an official role, such as clerk or professor. In order to *załatwić sprawę* within formal settings or outside of them, parties to the negotiation must be in a private relationship, either through a third person or through the rituals of etiquette.

Pan B. arranged for his secretary to type and photocopy his son's doctoral thesis. The son had expected to pay the woman in złoty for her work, but she refused to accept any money at all. The young man was upset and solicited his girlfriend's help in selecting an appropriate womanly gift. After careful consideration, he presented the secretary with nicely-adorned flowers, coffee, a bar of chocolate and a bottle of whiskey, all purchased in Pewex, a nationwide chain of stores where goods are sold for hard currency only.

The secretary did a favor for her boss's son. Had she accepted money, she would have been acting in her public role as a secretary. But because she did not accept money, she got herself into a private relationship with her boss.

Even if the secretary received a present worth more than the money offered, to equate the present to its monetary worth would be a breach of etiquette. Because presents are given only to private people and the secretary made herself a private person by refusing to accept the money, she now has much more bargaining power than if she had taken the money, even the large sum of 16,000 złoty (about a month's wages) offered. The boss is now indebted to his secretary simply because she did not accept cash payment. She can now expect favors from her boss in accordance with their private relationship.

The elaborate etiquette of *załatwić* enables people to sound one another out and proceed subtly in the making of informal economic arrangements, some of which are clearly illegal or semi-legal. For most people, *spekulacja* and "corruption" are social evils. Even so, almost everyone in everyday life is involved in it on a small scale and considers his activity normal and acceptable.

Laws against "corruption" and black market dealings are strict and criminal penalties are harsh, but the system's real rules are much more tolerant than its laws. Very few people are actually prosecuted for "economic crimes"—those who are, are prosecuted for small-scale illegal activities. Rarely are big operators—usually Polish millionaires, the so-called "fat fish"—prosecuted.

Sometimes illegal economic activities are used as a pretext to prosecute an individual—the real reason is not the stated one. In 1981, during the Solidarity period, representatives of the Prosecutor General's Office and of the Ministry of Justice, reported that, in 1980, 1,000 indictments were directed to the courts concerning serious economic offenses. In 1981 legal investigations were in progress against a number of former high-ranking officials, including four former ministers, seven former deputy ministers, five former first secretaries of voivodship (district) committees, and two former secretaries of voivodship committees.

The only one of the former high-ranking politicians whose case was brought to trial was Maciej

Szczepański, Communist Party head of the Committee for Radio and Television, a function equivalent to that of a cabinet member. He was charged with squandering state property valued at several million złoty and spending government money for private purposes.

In 1982, General Jaruzelski granted amnesty to all former high-ranking officials accused of economic crimes, along with some imprisoned Solidarity activists and criminals. Szczepański was released for "health reasons" after serving half of his sentence.

Though many engage in "semi-illegal" activities, people conceal such activities because they are vulnerable. At any point, a case could be made against them, and practically no one would come away clean from a close investigation. So people buy and sell dollars but talk of "green fabric" or "mint chocolates" in public or over the telephone.

Załatwianie spraw need not require prior scheming. Through friends and acquaintances, opportunities for exchange often arise spontaneously. Barbara, a working-class woman who lives in Lublin, told me how her family obtained their living room rug, a print of yellow, brown and green.

A man who lives in her town drove to Kowary, a small town in Silesia (a region in southern Poland). He bought the rug *na lewo* for 17,000 złoty, and sold it to Barbara's neighbors for 30,000 złoty. The neighbors had asked that he buy the rug, unavailable in Lublin, for their daughter who would soon marry. The father hauled the weighty rug from the apartment of the man who bought it to his family's apartment—a long distance. But after the daughter saw the rug she decided she did not want it.

Barbara's mother happened to visit the neighbors one day and heard them bemoaning the expensive purchase they could not use. Barbara's family decided to buy it. The neighbors charged 33,000 złoty for the rug itself and 1,000 złoty for carrying it. Barbara's family is proud of their new and impromptu purchase.

A breach of the acceptable boundaries of *na lewo* behavior, both in terms of what one attempts to *zała-twić* and in the way one tries to wangle, results in embarrassment, failure and possible prosecution. The secretary and I were successful because we established rapport and entered into private relationships with the store manager and the boss, respectively.

What One Sees Through the Back Door

A thorough appreciation of the necessity for *na lewo* arrangements requires an understanding of the workings of Poland's official economic system. Though Americans have heard for years that "Soviet-type economies are dysfunctional," this is not completely true in Poland. The system is shaky but continually stabilizes itself because the informal economy is integrated with the formal.

Officially, Poland has a two-tiered economic structure. The first and largest tier is the state socialized sector. Formally and legally, Poland has a state-controlled, centrally planned socialist economy; major economic decisions flow from the few people at the top. The second tier of the economy is the legal private sector, unique in its large size in Eastern Europe. Legal private enterprises are owned by individuals but registered with the state and taxable. In 1984 there were almost 470,000 private, non-agricultural enterprises in Poland. During the same year, the private sector produced more than one-fifth of the national income.

The legal private sector is dominated by agriculture, housing, small-scale industry and handicrafts. Of the nearly one-third of the population employed in it, 17 percent works in services and handicrafts, and 83 percent in agriculture.

In contrast to the profit-oriented businesses of the cities and towns and specialized farming, private agriculture is largely subsistence, often even poverty-stricken. Though agriculture was collectivized in the early postwar years, farmland was returned to its prior owners in 1956. Today, 90 percent of all farms are privately-owned and 85 percent of all farm workers are employed in them, but private farms comprise only 75 percent of all farm land area. Sixty percent of all privately owned farms are less than 12.4 acres; 60 percent of cooperative farms are between 250 to 1,000 acres; and 60 percent of state farms are over 2,400 acres.

The legal private sector contributes goods and services to the public sector. In 1984, the private sector was responsible for 52 percent of the building construction (calculated per cubic meter), and it completed 90 percent of all buildings under construction. Private enterprises in rural areas completed 66 percent of all newly constructed buildings. To ensure prompt completion of a hospital under construction, city officials might decide to subcontract various projects to private firms. They might calculate that it would take a government firm two or three years or even longer to complete the necessary sewage system. The city would pay more, but the job would likely be completed within a year.

The built-in incentive system renders private enterprises more efficient and responsible. In relative terms, employees in the private sector are overpaid, but there is no security attached to the enterprises they are employed by. Entrepreneurs can plan for no longer than two to three years. Stability and security are doubtful, so people make as much profit in as short a period as possible.

Official state prices are generally much lower than those for the same goods sold by legal private enterprises. In 1983, for example, women's leather knee-high boots sold for 3,000 to 4,000 złoty in state stores but for 10,000 to 15,000 złoty in legal private enterprises in state-owned shops. Likewise, non-leather ladies' shoes, which sold for 900 złoty in the state store, sold for 6,000 złoty in the legal private sector. Though the rationing system of 1982 and 1983 alloted only one pair of shoes per person each year, I was able to purchase a pair of snug winter boots from a private cobbler. There was no need for a ration coupon, but the price was high: 10,000 złoty, nearly the average monthly salary in Poland at that time, and two and one-half times the official price. Though prices are favorable in the socialized sector, it is the uneven and unpredictable state distribution system that renders consumption in the private sector generally more desirable and effective. Citizens laugh at Western inquiries about efficiency and shopping. A professor of law at Warsaw University told me, "I never expect to be able to buy anything in state stores. I am actually happy when I find something."

Legal private enterprise also exists in the service sector of the economy and includes medical cooperatives, some restaurants and taxi services and ice cream and hot dog stands. There are private shops which specialize in clothing, jewelry or handicrafts and all-purpose stores where a chance assortment of goods can be found. Candles appear next to shoes, crammed on a shelf with spare automobile parts, household gadgets and souvenirs from Yellowstone National Park. In response to consumer demand, legal private enterprise is growing. Warsaw even has several private travel agencies, providing a welcome relief from long waits at the train depot or at Orbis, the state travel agency.

Officially, legal private enterprises acquire raw materials from the state sector and sell products at officially fixed prices. Government regulations ostensibly limit the scope and activities of legal private enterprise. Yet it is nearly impossible to operate such an enterprise without acquiring and selling goods by illegal means and engaging in a fair amount of illegal activity. A private restaurant, for example, is unlikely to operate successfully without produce obtained on the black market.

A 1985 article in the official newspaper *Zdanie (Opinion)* describes how illegal activity can increase the profits of legal private enterprises:

> In Poland it is a public secret that when a private manufacturer delivers 100 brushes to a shop, in reality he delivers 1,000 (when fifty have been sold, he reports forty-nine, which are tax-free). In this way he evades taxation, and fortunately so, for otherwise he would have to wind down the business or the brush would cost three times as much and shop assistants would lose their jobs.

Legality and illegality also overlap in the government-sponsored system of hard currency bank accounts and stores through which the state intercepts hard currency from citizens. In addition to the standard state stores, the Polish government operates a network of Pewex retail outlets, where people can buy both domestic and imported goods for Western currencies only—mostly for U.S. dollars. At Pewex, customers gaze almost reverently at precious Swiss chocolates, French perfume, German wine, Viennese coffee, Bic razor blades, Toni hair rinse, Marlboro cigarettes and Polish vodka, all displayed on inaccessible counters.

Citizens of most Eastern bloc countries are unable to go abroad to work; but for Poles it is possible, and, from the Polish point of view, working abroad is very lucrative. The son of one acquaintance worked in Libya, where he earned $10,000 annually—which has many more times the buying power in Poland than in the West. Poles often seek work contacts abroad through relatives or through visiting Westerners.

Hard currency bank accounts became accessible to citizens in the 1970s and have become commonplace, as acknowledged in the official newspaper *Polityka (Politics):*

> In the 1970s the Finance Ministry launched a pioneering bid to estimate the hard currency resources possessed by Polish citizens. Most of the specialists agreed that there must be at least $2 billion in private hands in Poland but said that $4 or even $6 billion could not be ruled out either. It can be assumed that, as a result of the crisis, these resources are slowly eroding as the money is spent in Pewex or put in black market circulation. The hard currency reserves of the population are a natural supply source of the black market, which is immune to the swings in the passport and visa policies.
>
> This year [1984] deposits in Bank Pekao, which is the main hard currency bank for the population, reached the record high figure of half a billion dollars. In the first five months of the year new deposits totaled $160 million, including $90 million in cash.

Poles within the country obtain Western currencies from relatives abroad or through black market transactions. The official currency of Poland is the depreciated złoty, but dollars are a preferred medium of exchange for certain goods. Though people have become accustomed to the idea that commodities such as spare parts for automobiles and farm machinery, some medicines and apartments (without waiting) are often available only for Western currency, a friend expressed dismay when he saw a farmer quoting a dollar price for his eggs during the economic slump of 1982.

According to sources cited in a 1984 article in *Polityka,* the blackmarket trade in dollars is extensive and considerable:

> We do not know the exact scale of illegal hard currency turnover in Poland. Police headquarters estimate that some $80–120 million as well as two tons of gold change hands during one year now.
>
> The efficiency of combating the trade is negligible. In the first half of the year, the militia seized just over $400,000

from illicit deals, starting about a thousand investigations. Everybody knows that this is only the tip of the iceberg.

Despite various changes of recent years, the black market is alive and well and it could hardly be expected to be otherwise at a time when the difference between the official and the black market exchange rate of the dollar is one to five. You can't expect foreign visitors and Poles who own hard currency to act like fools. The cashiers from exchange counters that I talked to could not recall a single person turning up (of his own volition) to exchange dollars at a rate of 110 złoty [the official price of one dollar at the time].

Despite the increasing inflation of the 1980s, the price of the dollar has remained fairly constant. Two main factors determine its price: the price of cars and the price of Polish vodka in Pewex. (About 25 percent of Pewex sales are in Polish vodka.) An increase in the złoty price of vodka in state stores or the price of cars on the legal private market pushes up the price of the dollar, and vice-versa.

An interview with Pan Zygmunt K., black market dealer, in a 1984 article in *Polityka*, revealed the following:

Interviewer: How much do you pay for a dollar?
Pan K.: Today 580 złoty for a dollar and no more.
Interviewer: Not long ago it was more than 600 złoty.
Pan K.: Well, you should have sold them [dollars] then. This is the off-season. Some tourists have arrived, and it's easier to buy dollars.
Interviewer: That's why the price fell?
Pan K.: Not only. There's no demand now. Fewer people travel abroad [than in the 1970s]; buying cars by internal export isn't profitable ["internal export"—the selling for hard currency of cars offi-

cially imported by the state—is not profitable because prices are high, spare parts are unavailable, and gas is rationed]. It's true that the price of vodka in Pewex recently dropped, but buying vodka in Pewex is also not very profitable. And today, fewer and fewer people have money to invest in green [hard currency] without a definite goal. The market works normally. Prices depend on supply and demand and I am a broker who lives off a profit margin.

Interviewer: Supply, demand, profit margin—I see that you are an educated specialist.

Pan K.:   And you thought that I only finished fourth grade and have a crowbar up my sleeve.

Interviewer: And are there some [black market dealers] like that?

Pan K.:   Recently, some guys have turned up who steal from clients and cheat them in the exchange. That ruins business. Many people are afraid to engage in transactions with people they don't know. More and more, foreigners sell dollars through their host and guides. There are no licenses in this business. Everyone deals in hard currency. Do you know anyone who has never bought or sold hard currency for the black market price? I think most exchange is *załatwione* through amateurs who deal only sometimes, when the occasion arises. The possession of hard currency is not punishable. Our law punishes both those who buy and sell. If an undercover policeman denounced me because I sold him dol-

lars, he, too, would have to sit in
prison, according to the law. Of course
there is a risk, but doesn't a handicraft
worker who gives a bribe in order to
buy materials take a risk? The client is
as interested in secrecy as I am.

Poland had had a substantial illegal private sector,
and with the emerging decline of the state economy
at the end of the 1970s, this sector grew. The illegal
private sector helps to meet the country's basic food
production and distribution needs.

Individual farmers supply urban consumers with
meat and other staples directly, bypassing the state
purchasing agencies. Peasants park their vans or small
trucks and sell goods from the backs of their vehicles. They peddle produce, often alongside state food
stores, or in large private markets such as Rembertów, where one finds a mixture of legal and illegal
activities.

At Rembertów, an all-purpose market in Warsaw,
consumers pored over secondhand Beatles records,
Playboy magazines, microphones, batteries and an-
tiques. I bought a boot zipper unavailable in the state
stores from *spekulanci,* those engaging in *spekulacja.*
To complete my shopping at Rembertów, I bought
an English-Polish dictionary in a quality edition that
was difficult to locate elsewhere in the country. It is
said that Rembertów, teeming with people, is the best
place to search for practically anything unavailable
or scarce in state stores. The crammed buses head-
ing towards the marketplace attest to its popularity
among consumers. Even if a certain desired good fails
to materialize, some other long-sought treasure will
probably be found on market day at Rembertów.
Private marketplaces often, though not always, in time
provide desired scarce goods.

Though the terms "black market" and *spekulacja*
had conjured images of the underworld in my mind,

I soon learned that they do not necessarily occur in dingy side streets or in disreputable districts of town. Such activities are sometimes virtually open, taking place on well-travelled public sidewalks and over the telephone, in masked language, between respectable citizens. A *spekulant* is often looked down upon, but one who buys goods from him for socially-accepted ends is not.

I had assumed that legal and illegal activities were well-defined, yet Poles themselves were often unable to explain the lines of demarcation between the two. People operate in both legal and illegal levels of the system. In the mind of the average consumer, the distinctions are not only blurred, they are unimportant. As one friend pointed out, "Most Poles don't even know what the differences are, much less care or think about them."

A Polish television network broadcast a program comparing markets and stores of today with those of the 1960s. In a neutral tone, without condemning the practice, the announcer discussed the legal and "semilegal" *spekulacja* prevalent in the market place of the 1980s.

I asked another viewer to distinguish between the legal and perhaps not-so-legal activity shown on television. "Not even lawyers can tell you the difference," she told me. Legal and illegal activities operate alongside and in conjunction with one another.

What is legal is often not considered moral; what is illegal is often considered moral. In thinking about how to obtain quality medical care, acquire tickets for Jazz Jamboree, an annual international jazz festival in Warsaw, or emigrate—whether legally or illegally—people weigh moral and pragmatic concerns, but not legality. In a society in which people find it necessary to slight the system, the boundaries between legal and illegal are understandably fuzzy.

People often choose careers and jobs for the kinds of opportunities and resources they offer—perhaps contacts with foreigners, possible trips abroad, the siphoning off of goods, the use of state services for private ends. Pensions in some professions are relatively low, yet the legal benefits or opportunities to use learned skills in the private sector make these professions attractive. Teachers of mathematics, physics or foreign languages tutor pupils on an individual basis; physicians work in private sector cooperatives or treat patients privately.

At work, people are officially in their public roles, yet many of them profit from private arrangements that they are able to undertake because of resources accorded them by state jobs. The effectiveness of private arrangements often depends upon the resources of the state bureaucracy.

Writing in a 1984 article in *Życie Gospodarcze*, economist Marek Bednarski explained why employees often work for themselves during official working hours:

> In those trades for which escape into the informal economy is possible, material motivation is seriously weakened as the illicit income is far greater than the additional reward the enterprise can offer. Therefore the worker minimizes his effort, treating the job in the state enterprise mainly as a basis for qualifying for social insurance benefits and, often, as a source of free materials and orders. The wage then ceases to be the main motive for working.

A housing administration maintenance man may spend many of his official working hours fulfilling unofficial private orders which come to 150 to 200 percent of his official earnings. And a car mechanic in a state garage may repair cars *na lewo*, pocketing the fee which amounts to 100 to 120 percent of his daily earnings.

Shoemakers and tailors can use the materials and tools provided them by the state to make goods intended for private sale. If they had to procure such hard-to-come-by materials independently, their private activities would be nearly impossible. In many ways they are dependent on their state jobs for semi-secret and usually illegal businesses.

Officially, few are unemployed. According to official statistics, only 5,000 people registered as unemployed in 1984, while 262,000 positions went unfilled. Yet, if there is no unemployment in Poland, there is considerable underemployment. People speak of "being employed" at state jobs, but few speak of "working" in this context. A 1983 article in *Życie Warszawy (Warsaw Life)* reported on absenteeism in the Lenin Steelworks in Cracow. "Every day 10 percent of the workforce is out on sick leave."

The attitude towards state work is basically lackadaisical. The bulk of the adult population wakes up in the morning, rides the tram or the bus to work and officially, stays on the job for the prescribed amount of time. That the state media attempt to instill in the population a strict work ethic is reflected in the recent special on Polish television about the industriousness of the Japanese. The special emphasized that the Japanese people value work for its own sake, and that they work very hard, whether or not they see the benefits. But, in Poland, while those employed in state enterprises are entitled to retirement benefits and vacation privileges and state jobs allow workers to send their children to kindergarten, working hard on the job is not necessarily rewarded.

Fatigue and frustration are born of the waste of energy and time and the general inefficiency typical of the Polish workplace. Yet this does not mean that Poles are lazy. Workers often take breaks during working hours to go about the business of shopping and managing the household. I often tried to *załatwić* something—to buy an airline ticket, mail boxes abroad or pick up my ration cards—only to find that the low level bureaucratic workers, usually women, were out. Even the explanation that the absent bureaucrat is

"at dinner" may be a euphemism for something else—
a hopelessly long line for mineral water, which she
also may buy for work colleagues, or a protracted
wait with a sick child in a crowded, dingy hospital
hall for the doctor, who is off treating patients privately. And so there is a chain reaction; everybody
waits because everybody is out waiting.

Janusz, who designs engines, is ambitious and enjoys his line of work. He is eager to move forward
in his profession. But he finds the workplace demor-
alizing. On the average, his supervisor gives him and
his colleagues three months' time to accomplish one
month's work. He often finds himself ridiculed by
coworkers for asking for more work to keep himself
busy. Many of Janusz's fellow workers come to work
late, eat breakfast on the job and are already waiting
at the exit gate at 3:50 in the afternoon so as to leave
promptly when dismissed at 4:00.

Walking through the streets of Lublin with Barbara, a working class woman in her twenties, an attractive piece of material in the window of a fabric
store caught my eye. The sign *dekoracja* (decoration)
stood beside it. Barbara told me the sign meant "display only;" neither this piece of material, nor any
material at all, could be purchased in the store.

When I asked Barbara how the clerks occupy
themselves, she replied, "The clerks sit around, and
when a shipment of material does come in, maybe
once a week, or once every other week, they are very
busy selling everything from the shipment. But,
within several hours, they are free again."

I frequently saw similar situations. Sitting in the
dentist's chair, I overheard two dental assistants
complaining that, had it not been for the occasional
checking of their supervisor, they would not have to
come to work at all on Fridays. As they were preparing to leave at 3:45, a man came to arrange a dental appointment for the following week. Though the
office was technically open until 4:00, the reception-

ists officiously turned him away, saying they had "already closed the appointment books." Disgruntled, the man went away, knowing he would have to come back another day just to make an appointment.

Though little enthusiasm is typically evinced for state work, many people diligently work long hours at an unofficial job or at private activities to produce a second source of income, unreported to the government.

Barbara is employed as a clerical worker during the day. Several years ago, her brother and sister-in-law started their own part-time business, and now she has begun to work with them in the evenings. They make leather skirts on her sister-in-law's early-model Singer sewing machine and manufacture belts and bracelets. Barbara's brother, who pumps gas during the day, has plenty of extra fuel to travel around Poland in his car, buy leather *na lewo* and travel to various cities to resell the goods.

As an engineer, Janusz earns only 13,000 złoty per month, a few thousand złoty less than the average Polish salary. He is now considering taking on an extra job after working hours to supplement his income. He could drive a taxi privately, but this would entail considerable overhead. He could also work in construction for a private house builder or as a farm laborer in a village. Good heartedly, Janusz joked about his poverty: "My engineering job does have some rewards. Today there was a raffle at work, and I received four eggs!"

Because of unreported earnings, government figures on personal income are, at best, misleading. According to statistics compiled by the Central Statistical Office, in 1984 personal expenditures were 13 percent higher than personal income. An American scholar in Poland using only the statistics on income to compute standard of living was, for this reason, considered naive by his Polish colleagues. Writing in

1984 in *Życie Gospodarcze,* economist Marek Bednarski estimated that 10 to 13 percent of Polish personal income is derived from the informal economy.

So engrained in the Polish consciousness is the mentality of dual work that it is almost inconceivable to some that a country could function differently. A man who worked as a laborer unloading incoming ships at the port of Gdańsk for years siphoned off peanuts from the incoming shipments and exchanged them for various goods. In 1979, however, he left Gdańsk, seeking a better material life in West Germany. Settling in Hamburg, he was soon disillusioned. He could no longer make an additional profit from his job, which had become his sole source of support. He had nothing to trade for scarce goods and services.

Exchange in Poland is generally based on individual problem-solving strategies. A striking exception to the purely individual approach is the refrigerator "line committee," an *ad hoc* organization of individuals who have one thing in common—a hope to buy refrigerators and other goods.

Since demand for refrigerators far exceeds supply, consumers are not likely to be successful by simply arriving at a store and standing in line for a refrigerator, unless they have an unofficial exchange relationship with the store management or access to unofficial information about delivery schedules. Consumers without such privileges would have to maintain their place in line 24 hours a day for however long it might take for their turn to arrive—often weeks. Given these conditions, line committees have spontaneously arisen, organized and controlled solely by people who wish to buy refrigerators.

In order to get a refrigerator for the apartment he will inherit from his great aunt when she dies, Paweł voluntarily took part in a line committee.

Paweł heard about the line committee through

acquaintances, so one day he simply went to the refrigerator store. People connected with the line committee congregated outside to conduct unofficial business. The main activity was the control of a list of names of individuals who wanted to buy refrigerators. The list was made up of people in the order in which they had arrived at the state store. An average list might consist of 300 names; Paweł was number 440 when he signed up.

Deliveries of refrigerators to state stores are sporadic and no information on inventories or delivery schedules is publicly available. Deliveries take place from several times a week to once in six weeks. Anywhere from five to 60 refrigerators may be delivered in a given shipment.

Controlling the list requires time and cooperation from everyone whose name appears on it. Twice each day, at 10:00 A.M. and at 9:00 P.M. at Paweł's store, the roll call of all the names on the list is read off. This is called "verifying the list." People whose names appear on the list of the line committee choose the person who will read off the list for each roll call. This is usually the person who is first on the list at the moment. Of course, as soon as that person succeeds in buying his refrigerator, he is no longer on the list or a participant in the line committee.

If Paweł is unable to be present for a particular roll call, he sends a friend or family member to say, "I am here" when his name is read off. For, if no one were to speak for Paweł, his name would be automatically crossed off the list and added to the end. Missing only one roll call would cause him to lose his place.

But the line committee's work involves more than controlling the list. Even though a delivery of refrigerators arrives only every two weeks on the average, 18 people must stand guard in front of the refrigerator store round-the-clock. Vigilant groups are necessary to protect the integrity of the list by preventing people from barging into the store. Store managers do not honor the list.

So, in addition to roll call twice a day, Paweł has obligatory guard duty for three hours, roughly every third day. Though no information is officially available, individuals participating in the line committee do their best to find out when deliveries will arrive. They do this by developing relationships with clerks or with the store manager, who is sometimes tipped off about when deliveries will be made or how many refrigerators are scheduled to arrive. In exchange for information on delivery schedules and inventories, people connected with the line committee may tip the clerks or manager by doing favors or giving gifts such as flowers.

But the line committee is rarely privy to information that is completely reliable, and so the store must be guarded from potential line-jumpers. Round-the-clock, day after day, people on the committee's list take turns at guard duty. Pawel was on the list for four weeks, appearing for roll call and assuming guard duty, before there were any actual deliveries of refrigerators.

Any information about timing and number of refrigerators is of vital importance, for, when an individual is in the first 60 on the list, he is wise to stay after morning roll call in case a delivery materializes that day.

If a delivery materializes, those who have numbers one through about 60 are allowed by the others on the line committee to go into the store when sales begin, in the order they appear on the list. If only 20 or 30 refrigerators are delivered, the remaining 30 or 40 people will move up in the line and have more likelihood of success when the next delivery is made, perhaps in days or weeks.

Line committees have been formed not only among prospective refrigerator buyers. They also conserve time for and improve the success of prospective washing machine, sewing machine and other household appliance consumers. Line committees tend to be found in conjunction with the purchase of commodities that are unevenly distributed and in scarce supply.

But they are not reserved for hardware. Line committees have sprung up spontaneously in front of the Italian Embassy in Warsaw. Irena hoped to travel to Italy for two weeks during her summer vacation to visit her Italian boyfriend. She had already received a passport. She put her name on the list of the committee organizing entrance to the consular division of the Italian Embassy for Poles seeking visas to travel to Italy. The Italian Embassy issues only about 30 to 40 visas each day, and Irena had to compete for a visa with the hundreds of Poles who wanted to make summer pilgrimages to see the Pope. Irena became number 603 on the list when she signed up. A Ph.D. candidate in linguistics at Warsaw University, she complained that she had made little progress on her dissertation since beginning her pursuit of an Italian visa.

After the afternoon roll call one day, she paid me a visit. Exasperated, she told me she wanted to "resign from" both her dissertation and her trip to Italy. That day, nine big, burly men from the city of Wrocław had come to the Italian Embassy for the first time and barged their way in. The women of the line committee screamed and cursed at the men, and a physical fight broke out between some of the committee men and the nine outsiders, but, as Irena put it, "The guys from Wrocław were really huge." They all left with visas in hand.

Following the incident, Irena spent several hours comforting an elderly woman she had met in line. For the last two weeks the woman, from a small town four hours by bus from Warsaw, had been waking up each morning at 2:00 so she could board the 4:00

A.M. bus to Warsaw to arrive in time for the 9:00 roll call. She had expected to get her visa on the day the Wrocław men arrived, but, after their visit, she hysterically told Irena she would "never go on a pilgrimage to Italy," for which she said she had saved money all her life.

Line committees have over a ten-year tradition in Poland. They were originally inspired neither by Italian visas nor by material goods, but by a major cultural event. People clamoured to get tickets for *Konfrontacje,* an annual film festival in Warsaw in which the most famous world movies of the previous year are shown.

At its beginning in the early 1970s, *Konfrontacje* was held in only one theater with a limited number of seats. There were few showings of each film. People crowded the vicinity of the theater for several days before the box office opened. After several years, someone invented the idea of a line committee and people organized them.

In the latter half of the 1970s people seeking to buy household goods, such as furniture, tape recorders and bathtubs, began to use line committees.

In the "economic crisis" years of the early 1980s, line committees have spread to a variety of commodities. One line committee can go through hundreds of generations each year. They crop up where there is a shortage of a valuable commodity, one valuable enough to individuals that they will invest considerable time and other resources in order to procure them.

Informal solutions are not limited to legal activities. A neighbor hired a workman on a private basis to repair her window and paid him for replacement parts. When he was unable to obtain them from his workshop, he quietly removed them from the window of a client who did not employ him privately.

Other illegal activities are so usual that they need not be concealed. When a friend needed to have his telephone repaired, he called up the state telephone service. The woman who answered the telephone put his name on a list, but informed him it would be about six months before the repairman could come. My friend protested and asked for advice on how the job could be accomplished sooner. "Someone could come today, but only on a private basis. It would cost 600 złoty," said the woman. My friend's telephone got fixed that afternoon. The woman from the state services recommended an illegal solution over the telephone to someone she did not know. She had thereby arranged a job for her friend, the repairman.

The informal economy is so commonplace that some people will talk of everyday realities on the telephone. As a policewoman chatted with me, she mentioned a new book on the Pope and the late Cardinal Wyszyński. She lamented the steep price. She had heard that it cost 5,000 złoty "on the black market."

Everyday Know-How

Poles use numerous and varied means—informal and formal, legal and illegal—to obtain scarce resources. In a situation in which something is urgently needed but unavailable through state channels, it can usually be obtained if one has *dojście* (access through connections). One friend underscored this point: "You can *załatwić* anything in Poland."

The first task in operating successfully in the informal economy is to gather reliable information, to figure out who, how and where. People pump their networks for information on where and how to *załatwić* scarce resources and services, often asking everyone in the network, including family members, friends, acquaintances, colleagues and neighbors, for leads.

Ala told me how she managed to *załatwić* curtains. First, she systematically questioned immediate and extended family members, friends, neighbors and her wider circle of acquaintances. After several months she met an old high school colleague who sent her to a store where his aunt worked as a clerk. The aunt invited Ala to the warehouse, where she found curtains of all colors and varieties, not on display in the store itself. Ala made her selection and gave the aunt a tip for her kindness.

Though people generally receive information through networks of family and friends, they sometimes seek information in public settings, not only within a private circle. "Everyone asks everyone," said Ala in 1982. A woman I met once at a party whose father was dying of cancer asked me if I knew of someone travelling to Hungary. She had heard that a particular potentially-effective medicine unavailable in Poland could be purchased there.

In the marketplace or town square in the early 1980s, it became common to ask strangers for assistance since there were more scarce goods to try to locate. People halted passersby on the street to ask where they bought the toilet paper they were carrying. I was stopped several times myself. Once I was carrying an open box of Western goods received from friends in the diplomatic corps and was politely, but insistently, asked where I had obtained them.

I rode a crowded bus with Janusz at rush hour. When the seat next to me became vacant, Janusz came to sit down, but an elderly man nearby chided him that he should offer his seat to an elderly woman in accordance with Polish custom. Janusz had not seen her earlier and immediately gave up his seat. The woman soon noticed I was a foreigner, and, embarrassed that she had been so eager to sit down, tried to create a warm interaction. She told me she liked my skirt and asked where I bought it. This woman expressed her kindness by asking where she could buy something.

Individuals may question almost anyone for leads on how to obtain or accomplish something.

Getting information is neither direct nor simple. If one needs to solve a particular problem and does not already know an individual who can help, one lets the nature of the matter be known to acquaintances in various *środowiska*. If unable to help directly, these acquaintances will act as brokers, putting out feelers in their networks.

In the summer of 1984, a West German couple living in Poland needed to sell $200 on the black market for złoty. The black market rate had dropped because of the flood of foreigners vacationing in Poland that summer (following several years of nearly closed borders), and the couple had a hard time selling their dollars for 600 złoty each, previously the going rate. Among the people they asked for help was a friend of mine who had no need to buy dollars herself. She had heard from her godmother, though, that her godmother's sister wanted to buy dollars. Some acquaintances of the sister were putting on a wedding reception for their daughter and needed to buy $500 in order to purchase vodka for the affair. Through three intermediaries (my friend, her godmother and her godmother's sister), the parents of the bride-to-be bought $200, the maximum amount the West German couple wanted to sell (the parents had to *załatwić* the remaining $300 through other channels).

Once information has been gathered, a variety of solutions may be available to solve a particular problem. Janusz would like to buy chocolate for his brother's children. But chocolate is rationed and may be hard to come by even with ration cards. Ration cards for chocolate are available only for families with children, and one may have to wait in long lines to buy it. Many chocolate stores contain only empty shelves.

Since Janusz has no legitimate access to ration cards, he considers the following means: he could get chocolate by knowing someone or asking friends if they might be able to locate someone who works in a chocolate store with whom he could establish an exchange relationship; by exchanging one of his flour or cigarette ration cards with a friend for a chocolate ration card; by receiving chocolate as a gift or in exchange for a favor; by using some of the precious hard currency he is saving to buy a pair of jeans and purchasing chocolate in Pewex.

Strategies for obtaining medicines or medical supplies, some of which are in short or sporadic supply, are various as well. Scarce medicines that cannot be obtained over the counter in state drug stores might be acquired through these means: by having or developing an exchange relationship with someone who works in a drug store; through an exchange relationship with a well-connected physician who has access to certain medicines; by taking medicines from church relief supply stockpiles supplied by the West (usually facilitated by knowing a priest or church worker connected with the distribution of relief supplies); by asking someone travelling abroad or by writing to friends or relatives abroad to request that they bring back or send the medicines; by buying the medicine on the black market, usually for an inflated sum.

Often it is necessary to try a number of different avenues before one is successful. Obtaining books— or photocopies of books—creates a particular series of hardships for academics and professionals. Marketplace demand does not usually figure into the decision as to the number of books that will be published. There are no "best sellers."

A sudden rumor that a book in demand is available at a particular bookstore brings people hurrying to buy not only a copy for private use but also several extra copies for friends or for resale. During one of my university lectures, the professor announced he had seen a book for the course earlier that morning. He dismissed class immediately, hoping students could still buy the book.

Out-of-print books, even if not available in the library, are still not inaccessible. Pani Janina advised me to give a list of titles to a woman working in an *antykwariat* (used bookstore) along with a tip of 500 złoty. If the woman did not have the books, she would be pleased to extend herself, checking with other stores.

Janusz advised me to try photocopying hard-to-find books. Though most photocopy shops open to the public had been closed with the imposition of martial law, one shop in central Warsaw was said to be open. Dragging with me a bag full of books, I arrived early in the morning to avoid what I expected might otherwise be a long wait. But there was no line at all leading into the shop. Peering inside, I saw a cramped room with two outmoded manual copy machines. The one employee told me that the store was closed, indefinitely. The machines were broken, and no mechanic was available, she explained routinely. "The same repairman works on all the machines in Warsaw," she said. "They all broke down at once." She was uncertain when the shop would reopen and advised me to check back daily.

When I returned the following week, I knew long before reaching the shop that it had again opened its doors. People were lined up for blocks, clutching folders of papers. I would have had to wait the entire morning to use a machine—which might be broken by the time I got to it. I walked away from the shop, passing a line of people more patient than I.

A secretary in the Institute of Sociology told me it was possible the university could do the photocopying for me. The secretary would write a petition to the director of the library, authorizing the copying. I would need to have the petition signed by my academic advisor and the director of the institute, then stamped with the institute's seal.

Armed with a signed and stamped petition, I went to the library, happily anticipating that the matter was coming to an end and expecting to leave my books there for copying. But my joy was short-lived. I was told by the librarian, a kind and sympathetic man, that photocopying anything longer than an article was impossible. Several days later, only a part of the photocopying had been completed.

Finally, by chance, I found a solution with the help of a Warsaw University professor. In desperation, I queried him on how I could get books photocopied, and he advised me to go to a particular butcher shop. "Walk up to the third floor," he said. "There you will find a wiry man with a scar on his face. He's very gruff. After some polite talking, you can leave your books for him to photocopy. He'll not be happy to do it at first, but when you come back several days later with a considerable tip, he'll be in a much better mood."

Success in the informal economy is not guaranteed, even if a variety of solutions is tried. An acquaintance, who hoped to do his doctoral studies in computer science in the United States, came to me in desperation. He had been accepted unofficially by the computer science department at Massachusetts Institute of Technology, but, in order to be accepted in the university itself, he had to mail the completed application forms. It was not legal under martial law regulations to send such documents, even innocuous application forms, through the mail.

First, he asked if I knew someone who could aid him in smuggling the documents out of Poland; I was unable to help. Later, I heard, he got them out through an airline pilot, an acquaintance of his father.

But his trouble had only begun. Though he was admitted into MIT and even granted a scholarship, he had no passport. He tried to get permission for a "vacation to visit his uncle in Italy" but was denied at the passport office. Next, he tried a "vacation to visit his cousin in Africa," in both cases plotting to make a brief trip there and then go to the United States. To no avail.

Over coffee, he apologetically but intensely inquired, Did I have any advice as to how he could get out of Poland? But the hidden agenda was this, Did I know anyone who would marry him—on paper only—even for a considerable sum? He would be willing to pay several thousand dollars. Though he would never have asked me directly, he was hinting that I might be willing to marry him. I declined the indirect offer; I could suggest no one.

Success in solving problems through private exchange is aided by an individual's knowledge of the variety of solutions available, by the resources he has at his disposal and by his persistence in pursuing the options available. An individual can gain access to certain goods and services either by payment or through connections already in place. But he is less likely to develop an ongoing relationship with someone who simply sells black market medicine to him than he is with physicians, church workers or drug store managers who are family friends. The more connections are used, the more obligations are incurred with friends and acquaintances; relationships become long-term and binding, and those involved develop a social network insurance system.

Some people have become so accustomed to using informal channels, that they tend to think of the difference between informal and formal as a technical one. An official channel is just another channel. A friend related his observation about a small town in Poland: "During the crisis years of the early 1980s, people became accustomed to asking their friends and cousins to *załatwić* goods for them. Even after the market situation improved, they still asked their friends and cousins for help, even with goods that could be obtained through legal and official channels, directly from stores."

Not everyone has the same bargaining power in private arrangements or ability to choose between various options. An individual's status determines which of the solutions theoretically available within the system of private arrangements are actually available to him. As one friend humorously put it, "Everyone has an excuse for getting what he thinks he deserves. One says, 'My father is a veteran;' another says, 'I fought in the underground army;' the third says, 'I was the first in my class;' and yet another says, 'My former husband is a famous poet.' "

Privilege in *załatwianie spraw* need not be connected with class membership, family position or social achievement. Young married couples, for instance, are granted "credit" which entitles them to legal priority in buying household wares such as refrigerators and furniture. Veterans have the right to buy goods without waiting in line, to lower rent for apartments, lower taxes and priority in having telephones installed.

Both veterans and young married couples are free from the need to endure the rigors of line committees for refrigerators, as both groups have legal priority in buying them. These privileges are occasionally abused. Consumers high on the line committee list were outraged when a veteran who learned of a delivery arrived at a store where a line stood, and purchased a refrigerator at the official price. He then sold it at twice the official price outside the store in view of people whose names were on the line committee list.

Several categories of people are officially exempt from waiting in line for goods. Information is posted in all state stores that invalids, pregnant women and people carrying small children can be served without waiting. Interpretations of this policy vary. Often two lines are formed in a store—one for those exempt from waiting in line, the other for those without this privilege.

Class membership (intelligentsia, worker or peasant), membership in *środowiska* and family connections are statuses that create varying opportunities for negotiating private arrangements. Some networks provide more opportunities than others for private arrangements. Though strategies used in negotiation may be similar among the three groups, the goods and services exchanged often differ. Peasants are not likely to seek the latest "best sellers" (books) or tickets to fashionable theater; intelligentsia have no need for farm equipment.

Membership in or association with the Communist Party can be a resource in dealing in the informal economy. Pan B., who made his career in the Communist Party apparatus, is known by his friends and acquaintances as a person who has *dojście* (access through connections) and is particularly adept at solving problems. Pan B. serves as a liaison for people who have medical problems, simply because he knows how to gain access to physicians with particular medical specialties. He also knows where to turn to procure extra meat rations, buy a train ticket when tickets are sold out or come by an apartment for his niece. Though Pan B. is a particularly astute political operator—a specialist in networking—his success in developing exchange relationships and as an advocate is based on his former occupation, which placed him in networks providing optimal occasion for the negotiation of such arrangements.

☆　☆　☆

Everyone is, to some extent, involved in *załatwianie spraw*. The international aid officials I interviewed in

Poland generally operated according to accepted standards of "bureaucratic rationality." Many organizations had long lists of needy recipients and expected that those who received the goods would use them. But this was often not the case. Informal networks, not only the lists of bureaucrats, determine who ultimately receives goods. Those who received goods sometimes gave them to bosses, family members or friends as presents, or used them as barter items in exchange for something they needed more.

Though the massive relief effort undertaken by Western agencies, governments and churches provides help for many, it is necessary to understand the informal economic system to realize how goods are distributed and redistributed, that is, who actually receives them.

Poles play two roles—private and public—but they must be in private relationships in order to *załatwić sprawy*, even within the formal system. Informal patterns of organization are so visible in many arenas of economic activity that it is often difficult to recognize the formal structure.

The factors underlying the informal economy are complex. A 1984 article in *Polityka* cites several reasons for the "black economy" in socialist countries:

• First, services are relatively underdeveloped in comparison with the population's material resources.
• Second, large enterprises predominate, making the consumer's (buyer's) access to the producer or supplier of services difficult and causing protracted waits for commodities and services.
• Third, markets for particular goods are disorderly [and/or goods are generally in] short supply.
• Fourth, people desire additional incomes, earned more easily than they can on the official economy.

Clearly, the existence of the informal economy is related to a number of factors, including the chronic imbalance between demand and supply and the general ineffectiveness of the public sphere, including the ineffective market and system of management and planning.

In the West one often hears inquiries about why informal economic patterns are allowed to persist. The main explanation is that the government cannot control it: the informal structure does what the formal structure is unable to do. Without undercutting the state economy, the informal economy serves to satisfy consumer demands unmet by the state. Though, from time to time, the government declares a campaign of "fight with *spekulacja*," government measures are not effective in stopping such activities.

Puzzled, I asked Pani R. why the government tolerates informal economic activities. Amused by my question she replied half jokingly, "The government is like us; it depends on private exchange."

3

The Ties
That Bind

I met a group of Poland's "millionaires" at a
wedding in the city of Wrocław. Guests drove
to the church in Mercedes. Men wore tuxedos;
women attempted *haute couture* styles, with huge
jewels, lace, leather and silk. It was a group of young
entrepreneurs, many of them owners of boutiques.
They earned upwards of 20,000 złoty daily, more
than the average monthly salary in Poland. Over great
quantities of champagne and vodka, talk at the wedding party centered on business and money.

Poland's *nouveau riche* flourish despite the Polish
"crisis." A 1984 article in the *London Times* described
"The Champagne and Banana Set" well:

> The rich are not like us. For one thing, they eat bananas
> available only at two private markets in Warsaw at a cost
> of three pounds each. They go on package tours to Tur-
> key, to China (cost—close to a million złoty or seven years'
> average wages), to Vietnam, where the enterprising sell
> cigarettes and buy snakeskin to make into handbags. They
> buy their leather trousers and Hermes scarves from the
> Rembertów market, near the Soviet garrison, at Paris prices.
> Or they buy from private fashion collections.
>
> They use private helicopter taxis to take them from Cra-
> cow to their ski resorts—Zakopane, Bukowina or Szczyrk
> near the Czechoslovakian border.
>
> The truly skilled of the "banana youth" (as even the
> elderly rich are known) promenade down the main street
> of this once-charming mountain village challenging pas-
> sersby to take in their Swiss skis, their Polaroid sun-

glasses, their French zip up suits and Italian boots. Even the tan comes from Helena Rubinstein. After a while, it is time to rest in preparation for the party (a small p) ahead. The złoty millions are a fool's gold. As long as they stay in Poland, the millionaires are as rich as Croesus. Huge dachas are constructed with loving care. Inside, they bristle with video machines and kitchen mixers and hi-fi equipment. A man from the village does gardening, his wife cooks, his brother looks after the swimming pool, the grandmother is paid to queue for the meat, and the grandson cleans both the Volvo and Polski Fiat. As soon as the millionaire leaves Poland, the money trickles through his fingers.

Though many Poles cannot realize their consumer goals, some have ingeniously devised means to get much of what they want. (Millionaires are those who earn at least $35,000 yearly, which enables them to buy luxury apartments in the cities, elaborate villas in the country and expensive foreign automobiles.) A 1984 article in the official newspaper *Rzeczpospolita (Republic)* confirms that there are many Polish millionaires who have made their fortunes illegally:

> During only three quarters of this year, the prosecuting organs have uncovered over 700 such persons, whose combined property amounted to five billion złoty, which, by a simplified calculation, makes some seven million for each of them. Police data show that nearly 50 percent of inventors of similar good methods to get rich come from the private sector, while about 34 percent are employees of socialized [state] enterprises.

Westerners are struck by extremely well-dressed women, clad in fox furs and diamonds, parading the streets of major Polish cities. They may be members of Polish millionaire families who have earned their wealth through private enterprise, the underground economy, access to hard currency reserves, or earning-power abroad. According to a 1984 editorial in the Catholic weekly *Tygodnik Powszechny* (Universal Weekly),

Differences in wealth are not between private businessmen and public-sector workers, not between public-sector
workers and those in Polonian companies [small foreign
firms based in Poland limited to businessmen of Polish
background] nor between pop stars, actors, novelists or
filmmakers and those devoid of such rare talents, nor even
between our former or present leaders and all the rest—
no, the real differences in wealth are between those of us
who, with varying degrees of success, are trying to do
something in Poland and get paid in złoty, and those who
have been lucky enough to work for any length of time
abroad, anywhere abroad.

In contrast to millionaires, most Poles, including
professionals, lead more modest lives. However, this
does not mean they have no access to hard currency.

A film director travels frequently to Germany,
France and Switzerland to work in a theater. Though
his position and prestige as a theater director is much
lower in the West than in his homeland, hard currency earnings from abroad are valuable in Poland.
For two months' work in Paris one year he earned
$3,000. Exchanged on the black market in Poland,
this amounts to approximately one and half million
złoty, earnings of an average Pole over a 10-year
period. Commenting on the absurd comparison, he
laughed, "The whole country is without logic."

I played guitar and sang regularly with a Polish
group. When the neck of my guitar developed a crack,
Janusz said he knew a place where it could be fixed
before my next concert, just two weeks away.

A couple of days later he dropped by to say he
had made arrangements to have the work done. We
took a bus to the instrument-repair shop and went
through a back door, entering a warehouse cluttered
with various broken string instruments. A toothless
workman recognized Janusz and waded through the
cluttered mess smelling of glues and stale varnish to
welcome us. He found a dirty, rickety chair, and
covering it with an old newspaper, insisted that "the
lady" sit on it.

The workman discussed various techniques for fixing the guitar, but would not quote a price, saying he did not know how many hours of work would be required. Since the shop had no telephone, Janusz arranged to return the next week to check progress.

We returned the following week only to find the work unfinished. Several days later, we again took the bus to the shop and this time found the repairs completed. I offered the man what I considered a reasonable złoty sum, but he politely repeated how hard he had worked on the guitar, an indication he wanted to be paid in dollars. I added a $5 tip. The work had been completed before the concert and with skilled craftsmanship. It had required five separate trips to a distant repair shop and a payment in foreign currency.

Possession of hard currency offers the possibility to improve one's standard of living; life in Poland is full of contrasts.

Grażyna, a young physician, lives with her parents, grandmother, and brother's family in a cramped three-room apartment, plus kitchen and bath. Books, both classics and popular, line an entire wall, and along another wall is a new stereo and assortment of Western records. A persian rug, lamp draped with silk, dried bunches of flowers and modern art pictures decorate the room.

In order to get to her room, Grażyna must walk through the room her parents and grandmother share. She must also pass through the room her brother and his wife, both lawyers, and their young child share. It is furnished with a desk, bed, playpen and bassinette.

The one bathroom in the apartment is shared by six adults and contains no sink. Clothes soak in pails of water in the bathtub, waiting to be handwashed. Laundry hangs drying over the stove in one corner of the kitchen.

Barbara, a clerical worker, lives with her parents

in a poorly lit two-room apartment. She received her own apartment at a time when her married brother, his wife and son lived with Barbara's parents in their crowded apartment. She relinquished her apartment to her brother and family. Barbara sleeps on a couch in a pink room with a picture of Jesus on the wall. The room also houses the family's dining room table. Her parents and nephew, when he stays with them during the week, sleep in the second room, a room with dirty yellow walls, an early-model sewing machine covered with a white handmade doily, an old black-and-white television set and the rug purchased recently from the neighbors.

Janusz, the engineer, lives in a two-room apartment with his elderly mother. An all-purpose room serves as his mother's bedroom, as well as dining and living room. His cubby hole room filled with books is so small that when guests come to visit, he entertains them in his mother's room. Laundry hangs from the balcony, and the tiny bathroom doubles as a kitchen. The refrigerator is small and, in the winter, food is kept on the balcony.

Friends of Janusz, a young intellectual couple, have lived together with two young children in a one-room apartment (plus a small kitchen and bath) for 15 years. Since the energetic children play games during the day, the parents can study only at night. To avoid waking the children, the parents can not work in the main room. The husband, a university lecturer and specialist in the history of philosophy of India and Tibet, wrote his doctorate while sitting on the toilet, with the typewriter on his knees. The wife did her work in the kitchen. Under such conditions, she mastered three Finno-Ugrian languages, defended her dissertation and completed several books.

Janusz himself is expected to receive an apartment in three years. If he is single, he will get a studio apartment. If married, he will be eligible for a two-room apartment, but will have to wait longer to get it. He must inform the appropriate bureaucratic office if he will be married soon, so they can plan to give him a larger apartment. Agonizing over the situation, he wants to marry his girlfriend right away, but since she is not yet ready to make a permanent commitment, their relationship is strained.

For both rich and poor, life tends to become settled in Poland at an age that in the West generally would be considered fairly young. In contrast to the mobility of many Americans, Poles do not move around, either from city to city or from apartment to apartment. For years they wait for an apartment. Once they get it, they stay put. Piece by piece, young couples collect furniture and other material goods, some from parents, some obtained on "credit for young married couples." There are major life decisions, and those who make them have no illusions of staying "forever young." For Janusz, the studio apartment will be a permanent allocation, so he must pressure his girlfriend to decide about marriage quickly.

Poles have felt the effect of worsening economic circumstances in their deteriorating housing situation. On the average, more than one person lives in each room, and there are fewer people per room in urban Poland than in rural Poland.

The Central Statistical Office defines a household as a group of people living together, pooling financial and material resources and usually composed of relatives. This often includes family members beyond the immediate family who would not live together if given the choice. Over two-thirds of the households in Poland occupy an entire apartment; almost one-third share an apartment with at least one other household.

For many, quarters will become even more crowded. The housing shortage is increasing rapidly. Fewer and fewer apartments are being built in the 1980s. In both rural and urban areas, only about 80 percent of the total number of apartment buildings completed in 1978 were completed in 1984. Large state construction enterprises took almost twice as long to finish a housing complex in 1984 as in 1978. As a 1985 article in *Polityka* confirmed, "The state has generously promised apartments to everyone, but this gift, for which we pay money and wait 15 years or more, is moving farther and farther away."

In urban areas, approximately three-fourths of young, married couples are without apartments. In 1984, for every 850 apartments that became available for everyone seeking them, there were 1,000 newlyweds needing apartments.

Most often newlyweds live with parents or in-laws. With waits of 15 to 20 years for apartments, married couples with two children sometimes share two-room apartments with other relatives. Young people facing years of waiting speak of obtaining housing as "a miracle." In some cases, spouses live apart from each other for lack of space. The apartment shortage is so critical that a divorced acquaintance still shares an apartment with his ex-wife. Divorced couples often seek to exchange their larger apartments for two smaller ones.

Legally, an individual can have only one apartment registered in his name. Sometimes, people allow a younger relative to register as the legal occupant of an apartment to establish legal precedence should they die. A 24-year-old student, whose great aunt has already put her apartment in his name, said, "It's sad that I have to look forward to her death so that I can have an apartment."

Not only is living space limited but many Polish homes also lack modern facilities. According to the Central Statistical Office, in 1984 approximately 89 percent of the living quarters in urban Poland had a water supply; 77 percent had a private toilet; 74 percent had a shower or bathtub; 63 percent had a gas supply and 63 percent had central heating. In rural Poland, conditions were more primitive. Forty percent of living quarters had a water supply; 25 percent had an indoor toilet; 30 percent had a bathtub or shower; two percent had a gas supply and 21 percent had central heating.

The disparity between Polish conceptions of the "good life" and everyday realities has led to recurring unrest in Poland. The Polish government encouraged consumerism in the 1970s. At that time the policies of the government of Edward Gierek fueled consumer expectations beyond the production capacity of the country's industry and the distribution capabilities of the marketplace. In a 1984 poll conducted by the Polish government's Center for Public Opinion and Broadcasting Research, nearly 80 percent of those questioned termed 1971 to 1975 a positive period in Polish social history. Respondents cited the good market supplies and increased living standards of those years as reasons for their opinion. The expectations of Polish consumers rose steadily in the 1970s, but the economy could not keep pace.

Though, according to Poland's Central Statistical Office, the average monthly per capita income for wage earner's families increased by about 60 percent from 1981 to 1983 and for pensioner's families by about 74 percent during the same period, the general increase in wages did not keep pace with the soaring increase in the cost of living. Between 1980 and 1984 the cost of living rose by 357 percent for households of state employees, by 373 percent for peasant households and by 347 percent for pensioner's households.

Clearly, some groups have fared better than others in the "crisis." No official statistics can give a complete picture. According to a 1984 study conducted by the Polish Academy of Sciences:

> The actual wealth of people is made up of income from outside of the main work place, namely from moonlighting, from odd jobs done for private persons or for private

enterprises, from *spekulacja* and dealing in scarce goods, from selling hard currency earned abroad or received from family abroad.

In Poland, the distinction between the "haves" and the "have nots" is made by money and *dojscie* (access to connections). Those who do not *załatwić* are destined to live on society's margins. Pani Janina, retired woman from an elite family, wealthy before the war, talked of riches lost in the war, and admitted only with reluctance her difficulty in getting by:

> There are people in Poland—millionaires. But those—especially those who speculate—are engaged in dishonest work. Of course, for me it's not easy to live. You know, before the price increases, when I had 5,000 złoty monthly, it was enough for the necessities. And now I have 7,000 złoty, and it isn't enough.

In the first half of the 1980s, the cost of living increased by 55 percent more than personal income. "Economic crisis" has been used often in recent years to characterize precisely such a decline in the standard of living.

The disproportionate increase in the cost of living and personal income has resulted in a change in the structure of expenditures. Due to the failure of wage increases to keep up with price increases in recent years, Poles are being forced to spend an increasing portion of their income on food, and many have dipped into savings. The Central Statistical Office reports that from 1981 to 1984 expenditures for food increased by 126 percent in wage earner's households, and by 117 percent in pensioner's households. In 1984, "On the average, every third złoty was spent for food, every other złoty went for products other than food, while every seventh złoty went for alcohol."

The general standard of living has declined in recent years. Even so, Poles are accustomed to certain basic conditions. Despite cramped quarters and an apartment shortage, there are almost no homeless people. Despite shortages of medical supplies, everyone has access to medical care and insurance. Despite political instability, the rate of violent crime is low. Mothers leave babies in strollers outside of stores without worrying that someone will kidnap them. One can walk the streets of major cities alone at night. Many Poles are incredulous to learn that these conditions are not basic to many Western countries.

Possession of such scarce goods as apartments and cars have come to symbolize "prosperity." While visiting Poles, I was often asked how long one must wait for an apartment in the States, and if I had an apartment and car there. Owning a car in Poland indicates that the owner has done well for himself. Telephones, colored television sets, summer homes, abundant supplies of meat and spending vacations in a foreign (preferably Western) country also characterize the good life. Items such as expensive liquor, citrus fruits, nuts and raisins are also symbols of it and are considered excellent gifts in return for favors. Before leaving the United States in 1982, I asked Polish friends in California what gift would be most appropriate to take to the professor in Warsaw who was to serve as my academic advisor. They advised me to offer coffee: it is not too expensive and thereby in good taste, and it is "elegant."

Giving such gifts requires a certain tact and the proper circumstances. At the beginning of my stay in Poland I gave friends presents of American goods, such as Marlboro cigarettes. It was only later I learned they had called me "good aunt from America."

Though many Poles covet the enticing material goods and abundant opportunities associated with the West, prosperity Polish-style has its own peculiar ideals. The attainable Western material world for which Poles strive is one of cake mixes, Marlboro cigarettes and *Paris Match*.

When I visited Barbara for a weekend in Lublin, I brought gifts of coffee, Marlboro cigarettes, gum drops for her nephew and the German magazine, *Stern*. Very hospitable, Barbara in turn coaxed me to eat meat three times a day and to drink vodka and coffee together with her and her entire family. Her mother showered me with gifts of embroidered doilies and canned Russian fish, which a relative, a sailor, had brought back from his trip to the Soviet Union.

"Scarcity" does not mean that goods are unobtainable but rather that it takes considerable time and energy to procure them. Everyday life in Poland is wearing, especially for women, who often hold two full-time jobs—one at work, the other at home. Nearly half of the labor force is made up of women. An acquaintance of mine, a middle-aged female surgeon, spends full days in the hospital taking care of patients and supervising staff. Yet she does all of the shopping, housework and cooking and does not expect her husband, also a surgeon, to perform these household tasks.

A study carried out by sociologist Edmund Wnuk-Lipiński showed that working women spend an average of 6.5 hours on their jobs and 4.3 hours on household chores and shopping each day. In sharp contrast, men spend 7.5 hours at work and 1.5 hours doing household tasks. Women who do not hold jobs spend 8.1 hours each day carrying out household-related duties.

Maintaining the household is so time-consuming that even children must help by standing in the long lines for food and coveted goods such as refrigerators, carpets, books, televisions, tape recorders, shoes and nice clothes. According to officials at the Central Statistical Office, more family members now spend time standing in line than before the "crisis." People rely on family members, who share responsibility for arranging job promotions, obtaining rationed gasoline and standing in line for basic food and supplies.

FAMILIAL SOCIETY

On one occasion, Barbara insisted I come with her to a dance she and coworkers had planned. Plump and plain-looking, she typically wore a simple A-line skirt, ill-matched blouse, hose or anklets and high heels, both at home and to her office.

Barbara delighted in knowing an American and was eager for me to visit her as often as possible. She wanted to show me off to family and friends.

Conscious of tradition and social etiquette among her peers, Barbara worried that, as commonly happens, too few men would be present at the party, so she arranged a date for me. Her cousin, serving his two years of required military service in the army, was stationed near Barbara's home. He had agreed to be my escort and had obtained a pass for the occasion. When he did not appear on the evening of the dance, Barbara frantically tried to telephone him. When she finally reached him, he explained that all passes to leave the compound had been blocked at the last minute, because a counterfeit pass had been found in the possession of a recruit.

On the phone, Barbara pleaded with her cousin to *kombinować* (scheme—to devise an ingenious, possibly devious solution) until her mother, standing nearby, warned her that the army is "no joke," and he could get into serious trouble for such shenanigans. Embarrassed that her long-awaited friend from America had arrived and she couldn't supply me with an escort, Barbara pressed her mother, a janitor in the Officer's Club in Lublin, to do something.

Her mother telephoned an officer she knew from

the club. Profusely apologetic, excusing herself several times for having disturbed him, she explained that her nephew had had a pass to leave the compound. His ailing 85-year-old grandfather from "another corner of Poland" had come to visit and was leaving the next day. "This will likely be the last time he can see his grandson," she insisted.

Happy to do a good deed, the officer assured Barbara's mother, "He'll get it right away, right away." Delighted with her success, Barbara's mother proudly told and retold the story to relatives in the apartment below. The cousin arrived, shortly after the mother's small triumph, and changed from his uniform into street clothes. As we walked out the door, Barbara's mother told us to have a good time but warned her nephew not to return drunk to his compound the following morning.

Informal social networks, family-based and extending outward into specific circles, are the mechanism which enables the whole private informal system to work. In order to survive in an economy of scarcity, family members in Poland form a socio-economic unit, helping one another negotiate private arrangements in an informal economic system. Relatives, whether or not they care for physical or personal closeness, cannot afford to disown one another, political affiliations and views notwithstanding.

Family members can do a number of things to maximize their resources and thereby increase their ability to negotiate outside exchanges. Better-educated parents often encourage their children to go into service professions, such as medicine and dentistry. Networks are more important than wages. Though salaries are relatively low, professionals of this type can develop valuable exchange relationships with patients or, in addition to their state jobs, work in lucrative medical cooperatives, or have private practices. Other professions that pay relatively well are the military and the police, good for both salary and benefits, and almost any kind of private enterprise, most notably clothes, handicraft and jewelry boutiques.

Family members often pool resources when negotiating daily exchanges. Grażyna's parents encouraged her to become a medical doctor, and their daughter's profession is now an asset to them. Grażyna furnishes prescriptions and medicines for members of her household and more distant relatives. And, in exchange for her work as a medical practitioner, Grażyna obtains fabric from clerks who work in fabric stores and Western medicines from church functionaries who distribute international aid supplies. For the same reason, she and her family enjoy a broadened circle of acquaintances—including contact with an intellectually elite group of famous writers and artists—who bring her and her family a heightened social status, a resource in itself.

In many cases, more economically powerful members of families share resources with the less powerful. Though young adults often express a desire to be independent, their main financial and material support comes from the family. Central Statistical Office findings published in 1984 indicate:

> The material situation of young couples is bad, as testified to by the fact that one-third of low-income families (up to 3,000 złoty per capita) last year were young families. Over half of the young couples relied on assistance from friends or relatives.

One 29-year-old professional told me, "My grandmother still helps my mother by lending her money when she needs it. My grandmother cancels the debt when my mother cannot repay her. If my mother gets relief goods from the West, she gives them to my grandmother or to me. When I get a relief package, I give something to each family member, including my grandmother and my girlfriend."

In being with young adults in Poland, professionals and working class alike, I was struck by their financial dependence on and personal closeness to their parents. Despite her tight finances, Pani Janina takes responsibility for her fortyish daughter and grandson by preparing daily dinners for them and borrowing money from relatives when her daughter needs help. Pani Janina was shocked when I told her that children in their twenties in the United States often become financially and otherwise independent of their parents, even if the parents can afford to support their children. "But parents exist in order to help their children," she said.

Marriage is an important choice, both for personal reasons and career and material considerations. Many people get their first jobs through family connections. One individual told me, "Before people get married, they look closely at the parents of their respective spouse to see what the parents can do for them."

Young married couples depend on parents not only for material help but also for help in childcare and maintenance of the household. Maternal grandparents often play a special role in maintaining the household of their daughter and caring for her children. If the home of the maternal grandparents is a great distance from the mother's established home and job, the grandmother or grandparents may visit during vacation times in order to care for the grandchildren. A non-working grandmother may visit for longer periods and assume responsibility for childcare. In one survey, nearly two-thirds of women and more than one third of men who were parents of married children said they continually helped their daughter with tasks related to maintaining a household. Nearly one-third of grandparents surveyed take care of their grandchildren on a daily basis. Grandparents often invite grandchildren to visit for several weeks or months during vacation periods.

In Poland children are a source of prestige. Not

only parents but also relatives and friends put time and energy into caring for them. Many parents have much vacation time off from work and are able to spend more time with their children. In a society where family ties are paramount, there is considerable pressure to have children. Children of single women are often cared for by the women's mothers. It is socially acceptable in some *środowiska* to have children out of wedlock, and one out of ten mothers are single. Though unmarried, Ala decided to have a child. Her mother came to visit for several months at a time to help her take care of the child. All three went on extended vacations together to the countryside. Ala will take a three-year paid maternity leave from work. She prefers to raise the child herself, rather than taking it to a state-operated nursery.

The attitude towards children reflects the idea that, no matter what the situation, "you must establish your family." The dramatic increase in the birth rate which began in the Solidarity period and continued to climb through martial law cannot be explained solely on the basis of the postwar generation coming of childbearing age or on reduced entertainment during martial law.

A spokesman for the Central Statistical Office told me that Poland's birth rate was seven percent higher in 1983 than had been predicted on the basis of such factors as the number of women of childbearing age. During that year, one-fifth of all births in Europe (excluding the Soviet Union) occurred in Poland. A high birth rate continues.

Siblings, with or without children of their own, share the responsibilities of childcare. Four days of the week, Barbara and her mother take care of Barbara's nephew. Only on weekends does he return home to his parents.

Before adulthood and extending into it, young people depend on parents for material support. Generally, they are beneficiaries of the system, not yet its manipulators. But, as they grow older, they assume more responsibility for parents and grandparents. About two-thirds of Poles over 60 years of age currently live with their children.

In Poland "the family" may include extended family members such as aunts, uncles and cousins, or the term may refer to immediate family members—children, parents, sometimes grandparents, often people who share a household. People speak of "the closest family," which is defined as either of the above. They speak of "more distant family," those wider kin relations with whom they may or may not have frequent contact.

Cooperation between family members in urban areas is of utmost importance in managing everyday life. For instance, Barbara explained how she plans to go about obtaining a refrigerator when she eventually moves into her brother's apartment. (Line committees do not exist in Barbara's area.) "I'll tell everyone that I need a refrigerator, since I never know which of my friends will be able to załatwić it," she said. "I'll talk to everyone to avoid the situation somebody could get the refrigerator but doesn't know that I need it; maybe somebody will find it and in the meantime I can załatwić something for him."

"But on whom can you most depend to help you get the refrigerator?" I inquired.

"Well, on my family. Always."

"Family, meaning your parents and brother?"

"No, no," she adamantly replied. "Family means the closest family. Brothers and sisters of my mother, their husbands, their families, the family on my father's side. We can really count on each other."

Barbara depends not only on her parents and brother and his in-laws but also on her entire extended family unit. It would be to Barbara's advantage if a family member were able to załatwić the refrigerator directly, but if this is not possible, she will have to rely on friends and acquaintances.

"What would you have to do for them if one of your friends or acquaintances actually managed to *załatwić* the refrigerator for you?" I inquired.

Barbara mused: "Usually, I am told what kind of tip the person in question wants—vodka, coffee or something else. Then I say, 'OK, I have coffee, but please *załatwić* the refrigerator.' Of course, I can say that I have no coffee, but then he will say, 'I have no refrigerator.' "

"Is it always like this? Is reciprocity always required?" I asked.

"The further away one gets from the family and close friends, to distant acquaintances, the harder it becomes to *załatwić*," Barbara replied.

Though reciprocity is demanded outside the inner circle of the family and close friends, exchanges within family, such as Barbara's, are implicit. Families assume mutual help—that family members will do favors for each other and receive only "thank you" and respect in return.

Family members living in urban areas often exchange with those in villages. Many peasants have urban relatives. The government's social policy of transferring the labor force from agriculture to industry resulted in postwar migration to urban areas. Though, before World War II, 65 percent of the populace resided in rural areas, now 65 percent lives in towns and cities. Exchange relationships carried on between urban family members and their country cousins can be important for all concerned. For cultural reasons, peasants do not usually have acquaintances in the city, and, therefore, it is difficult for them to *załatwić sprawy* there unless they have family connections. Farmers, in turn, provide their urban relatives with fresh farm produce.

Many urbanites have relatives in villages, but some are reluctant to admit this. Pan B. allows his close friends to meet his father from the village, but not his boss or colleagues from work. Pan B's father helped Pan B's boss *załatwić sprawy* in the village. Yet Pan B. did not invite his father to his namesday party at home to which he extended invitations to work associates. "My father talks in villagese," he said.

Though some city dwellers may be ashamed of having rural relatives, using these contacts has become a matter of economic necessity in recent years. The aunt of Ala's mother has a small farm. During the food crisis of 1981 to 1982, Ala visited her relatives every two weeks in the spring and summer and every month in the fall and winter. Ala brought coffee, tea, and cocoa sent from her sister in London. The mother's aunt supplied Ala and her daughter with eggs, cheese and cream from her own farm and meat from the farm of a neighbor. "They were a great help during the worst times," Ala commented.

Before the economic slump, urbanites had more contact with their urban relatives than with their rural relatives. Now, however, urbanites often seek out relatives in villages because they make good exchange partners. Urban dwellers can *załatwić* refrigerators, cars, tractors and spare parts necessary for farming. They can also bring store goods such as batteries and light bulbs. Villagers offer chicken, pork, milk, eggs, and other farm produce. While city folk formerly visited village relatives to pick fruit, they now go for staples and often for vacations, which have become more expensive. Because of the uneven and unpredictable market distribution system in various localities and periodic shortages of basic food staples, most notable in the years 1980 to 1982, extended family members residing in other regions often make better exchange partners than those closer to home.

How resilient is the Polish family? Under what circumstances do families break up? Which family relationships—marriage, parent-child, brother-sister, wider kin—most often break up? Are differences cultural or personal?

The family relationship which crumbles most often is marriage. Though divorce in Poland is not difficult legally or bureaucratically, it is very expensive, and couples who get divorced are often forced to live together after divorce because of the apartment shortage. The Catholic Church does not have a significant influence in discouraging divorce. One church spokesman underscored this point: "No one thinks the Church's stance on divorce significantly decreases the number of divorces."

After divorce, children usually live with their mothers, sometimes together with the mother's parents. Grandmothers and maternal aunts generally assume some, if not considerable, responsibility in childcare. Such children often maintain contact with their father and his relatives, but paternal relatives usually help less than maternal ones in nurturing and providing material support.

Parent-child relationships are severed only in rare instances. Close contacts are maintained despite ideological and political differences. Under the tense and uncertain conditions of martial law, some spoke of wrenching political disagreements with family members. A 29-year-old described his conflict "of a political nature" with his mother but concluded in the next breath, "In spite of everything families stick together in one way or another. I don't know of anyone really separated from his family because of political differences." Another young adult commented, "I don't know anyone who doesn't see his parents, even if the relationship is conflict-ridden."

To what extent do people call on distant relatives for assistance in exchange matters? Middle-aged Pan B., who claims he has about 50 "cousins," says he is regularly in contact with five of them. Occasionally, he will make contact with the others when "I need to be in contact." Whether an individual claims a particular cousin as part of his family tree may depend on his exchange needs and purposes. Pan B.

uses the blood relation as an "in," enabling him to bypass the initial etiquette of *załatwić*. Family boundaries may be manipulatable and situational.

The family can be defined narrowly or broadly, and people often conceive of it in operational terms. Those who have no living close family members and the few who have little contact with family often consider *przyjaciele* (close friends) as family. Close friends become "just like in the family." Among workers and peasants, family usually plays the most important role in economy and exchange; among the intelligentsia, close friends are often more important in problem solving.

"The family" is not necessarily derived from a blood group. What is important is that an individual has a defined circle of people around him who perform the duties of family members. People who consider themselves to be a family operate as little islands, allocating resources unto themselves. Exchanges within the family are long-term, implicit and carry with them moral obligations, a promise of reciprocated support. Those without a family circle are truly disadvantaged.

* * *

Life in urban Poland is organized around two centers, the home and the workplace. Social life revolves around celebrations, often doused with a good deal of drink. Christmas, the most important holiday, is a family festivity. Both the first and second days of Christmas are celebrated at home, together with family members. Easter is also family-centered. Namesday parties, as important as birthdays, are celebrated both at home and at work.

Apart from family, in general Poles maintain contact with *przyjaciele* (close friends), *koledzy* (colleagues from school, work or other common experiences) and *znajomi* (acquaintances). Friendships and *znajomości* (acquaintances who can help one to obtain or accomplish something) are a form of insurance.

It is difficult to imagine life in Poland without close friends. Polish sociologist Stefan Nowak compares American "friends" with Polish *przyjaciele:*

> When Americans say about someone "he is my best friend," at the most we can say that the Polish equivalent of that is "good acquaintance." That which would correspond with friendship in our understanding is simply lacking in many cultures. To our friends we can go for help in many difficult situations and, in relation to them, we are obligated to offer help. A lot of Poles would go very far both in their expectations of real help and in terms of offering such help to their friends. Having a circle of *przyjaciele* increases the feeling of safety, both in psychological as well as in very "practical" aspects of life.

Outside of their families, people have relationships within their *środowiska.* A friend of mine, a dentist, socializes with dentists of her rank, intellectuals, artists and professionals and members of the church choir in which she sings. *Środowisko* refers either to a circle of friends or to a circle that would provide appropriate acquaintances, colleagues and friends brought together by profession. Those of one *środowisko* consider themselves social equals, though relationships within their circle may vary in intimacy. The dentist's friends belong to several different *środowiska,* and she meets with them separately. People of varying *środowiska* do not mix in private life, nor do they address each other by *ty,* the familiar form of you.

Środowiska are often separated. Since, as an outsider, I can glide through many more of them than a Pole, I was embarrassed on several occasions when I was with a person of one *środowisko* and chanced to meet a person of another. My contact with both parties was friendly, but it was strained, awkward and embarrassing for them to be put into an apparent situation of camaraderie with each other. It is the *środowisko* one belongs to that indicates who one's friends are, who one's potential friends may be and how one will act.

Koledzy are colleagues brought together by formal organizations or common experience. *Koledzy* can be close friends—often those with whom one forms lasting bonds. But *koledzy* and *koleżanki* (the female form of *koledzy*) are also everyone with whom one works, even if one started work one week ago. *Koledzy* are relationships formed through an institutional base or common experience. Hence, school girls have *koledzy* or *koleżanki* from school; university students have *koledzy* or *koleżanki* from the university; most adults have *koledzy* or *koleżanki* from work; many people over 50 have *koledzy* or *koleżanki* from the war or the resistance; and almost all males 18 years of age and older have *koledzy* from the army. People are *koledzy* and *koleżanki* for life, years after the formal organization or common experience that first made them so no longer brings them together.

Poles who lived through the war together, comrades in the underground or the Warsaw uprising developed special *koledzy* relationships. *Koledzy* and *koleżanki* from school or work from days past often operate as "old boy networks," relying on each other to solve problems. Though *koledzy* and *przyjaciele* are people through whom one can *załatwić sprawy*, these relationships are often of a moral quality, as in family relationships. *Koledzy* may now be engaged in vastly different pursuits, yet they continue to meet, getting together for drinking parties, reunions and namesday celebrations. In some cases their ties may be even stronger than kin ties.

A 50-year-old professor of mathematics still meets frequently with her *koleżanki* from secondary school for coffee klatsch and namesday celebrations. She has a higher position than her *koleżanki*, but they all belong to one *środowisko*. Likewise, a 62-year-old working class man meets often with his *koledzy* from a World War II underground resistance organization. The younger generation's counterpart of *"koledzy* from the war" are those relationships formed through working for Solidarity. In both cases, the cause changed the social relations of its participants. Many of those intensely involved in the activities of the Solidarity period, like members of their parents' generation, formed lasting bonds with *koledzy*. They discarded hierarchical barriers and called each other by *ty*, even across generational lines. One former internee told of the "interesting people"—writers, scholars, artists—whom he would not have met if not for his internment. His internment strengthened his association with the opposition and secured his access to opposition circles. Interned through the first months of martial law, this acquaintance told me:

> We were all on a first name basis. Not from the very beginning, all of us, but most of us; and after a week, we were all on a first name basis. . . . And we helped each other a lot. If somebody got a parcel from home, got food from home, it was shared, of course. It was not hidden. We shared everything—cigarettes—everything. . . .

In the beginning of martial law, those interned had such an intense experience that they became close *koledzy*, or *przyjaciele*.

> The first week, yes, we talked about politics. And we were all very frustrated and angry. The cell was extremely small and 11 persons in a place like that . . . There's a real tension, pressure—people don't know when they will be allowed out. Or how long it's going to last or what the next day will bring. Most of us, including myself, expected Russian invasion. It was after the miners were killed at the coal mine. And we expected a kind of national insurrection or other fights around Poland, even if not an insurrection. And we expected the Soviet army to come and calm the country down. . . .
> We talked about it with the guards. We asked them if they would release us if the Soviet army came, because

we were sure, if the Soviet army came, it would kill us all in a place like Białołęka [a prison] *all* internees, because we were the most dangerous. So we talked about their [the guards] releasing us if the Soviet army came. Nobody said "Yes, we'll release you," but nobody said, "No, I won't." There was a kind of psychosis and general paranoia in the prison.

The people that I spent the first hours with in prison— that I was in the same cell with—we will be friends for life. Within five hours we became *przyjaciele*; I am closer to them than others I have known for years.

Those who worked together in the underground after the declaration of martial law likewise developed close relationships. Those who lost their jobs for political reasons continued to meet, even though they no longer worked together.

The most distant relationships are those of *znajomi* (acquaintances). *Znajomi* has a broad meaning; it can refer to people that one sees frequently, or to those one has just met. Neighbors often become close acquaintances, aided by their proximity and the long time period, often years, in which they have to build relationships and engage in exchange. Hence there are "close" and "distant" acquaintances, as well as long-term and short-term acquaintances.

"Acquaintanceship" can be a handy category. For once two people have established contact, they can call upon each other at any time if the need arises. Their friendship can be reactivated, even if they have not seen each other for many years. Sociologist Stefan Nowak explained how such contacts help the state economy to function:

> Each manager in industry knows that cooperation with other factories or high-level administration works much better and is significantly more effective if the contact person is a *przyjaciel* [close friend] or a good *znajomy* [acquaintance].

People make available their own networks to others within their network. Through my friend Grażyna, I was able to avail myself of the services of her friend Dorota's father, even though Dorota was only a slight acquaintance of mine. I went with Grażyna to visit Dorota, who lives in a small town not far from Warsaw. Grażyna brought along with her two cartons full of old books that she wanted rebound. In his spare time Dorota's father binds books at home. He buys materials for his work *na lewo*. He keeps all the materials for this in the cramped quarters of the two-room apartment in which he, his wife and their thirtyish, unmarried daughter, Dorota, live. Grażyna had told me that Dorota's father does bookbinding and had offered his services to me in advance, so I brought along with me several old books to be rebound. When Grażyna and I arrived, a priest from a local parish was visiting with Dorota's father. He had also brought books to be bound. Dorota's father fulfills many orders from priests who serve the local parish.

Grażyna and I were to spend the day together with Dorota in her town. In addition to the food she had made for us and the books to be bound, Grażyna brought along several different kinds of cheap French perfume her mother had brought back from a recent trip to Paris. Grażyna brought five or six boxes of the perfume. Dorota's father will in turn sell them at his current workplace for 250 or 400 złoty, depending on the bottle. The women "clamor to buy the perfume," he said. "Paris" is written on it.

Informal exchanges are linked to family and friendship connections. In addition to spending time with one's inner circle of friends, which is a matter of honor and obligation in friendship, doing favors for friends deepens relationships. An acquaintance of mine, a grandmotherly woman in dowdy, mismatched clothes, rang up a price lower than the official one in the drab state-owned store where she works. Thinking it an oversight, I pointed out the discrepancy.

"It's all right," she whispered with a gleam in her

eye. This woman knew I was American and could afford to pay the relatively modest sum for chocolate candies. She had not undercharged me because she thought I had little money or because she considered the price of the candy exorbitant. She had taken the opportunity to show me she liked me; it was a gesture of friendship.

I learned that it is precisely this kind of teamwork that allows Poles to cope with such a loose and uncertain system. In the face of daily trials, people look to their families and *środowiska* for satisfaction and stability. As Ala expressed: "Five years without *znajomości* would be the biggest punishment in Poland."

One characteristic of exchange relationships is that exact equivalence of favors is almost never achieved because people maintain imbalances on purpose. Exchanges among friends and acquaintances are not simple barter transactions. They entail a system of obligations, often ongoing. People cultivate indebtedness to each other that can be used in the future.

Elżbieta, the daughter of an officer in the Polish army, wished to have a church wedding. Her father knew his career might be jeopardized if it became known that his daughter had been married in a church. In order to placate her without risking his own rank or reputation, the officer asked Pani Janina, who has relatives in a remote district of Cracow, to arrange the wedding in that district. The religious wedding would remain an unpublicized event. Pani Janina set up the wedding, knowing the army officer would *załatwić* something for her in turn—perhaps private quarters in an exclusive vacation resort or gasoline beyond the monthly ration for her husband or even help in securing a promotion for her son at work.

The debts people have to one another—like that of the army officer to Pani Janina—are deliberately unspecific. Pani Janina can "cash in" her credit with the officer at some future time, even after 15 years.

People are loyal to one another for favors, and it is precisely these loyalties and the implicit trust they entail that perpetuate the system of private arrangements. The officer, if he wishes to continue his relationship with Pani Janina, will arrange an exchange or locate a good for her, thereby creating an obligation on her part. Though private arrangements demand reciprocity, the terms of agreement are subtle. The value of exchanges cannot be quantified.

The obligations incurred by individuals in exchange—levels of giving and rate of return—often remain ambiguous and are conceived of only in general terms, yet the penalty for not honoring the obligations of friendship (and reciprocity) is loss of reputation, goodwill and, possibly, money. When Pani Janina needed some medicine, unavailable over the counter, for her sister-in-law's elderly mother, she called up an acquaintance who is a volunteer worker in relief distribution of medicines from abroad. The relief volunteer promised Pani Janina she would try to *załatwić* the medicine and call her back the following day. When the relief volunteer had failed to return the call two days later, Pani Janina complained, "When she needed me to *załatwić* something for her son, I did it immediately. But she is unconcerned when I urgently need something." Pani Janina concluded that her acquaintance is not a "friendly" person. The reputation and goodwill of the acquaintance suffered, since she did not fulfill the obligation of reciprocity.

Likewise, if the cousin of a physician is ill and needs the physician's "help" in securing a hospital bed, family members will be offended if he does not use his *dojście* (access through connections) towards this end. They might question his morality.

The terms of exchange are unequal between people who do not belong to the same *środowisko*.

A Pole desiring to establish a private relationship

with his boss can do so by doing a favor for him. For example, he could arrange channels for him to get meat from the village or take a typing job for his son. Likewise, if it is in the best interest of the boss for his employee to work on the job, it will likely be in his best interest to establish a private relationship with the employee, since many state jobs do not build in incentives for hard work.

For example, a professor at the university is on very friendly terms with her secretary. While on vacation in Romania and Bulgaria, they have met several times, the professor taking the secretary out to dinner. The secretary did not elect to take a sick leave from work (to the amazement of her physician) even when she was quite ill. She felt obligated to finish a typing job, even working overtime without extra pay, to meet her boss's deadline. Despite their affection and respect for one another, they will remain members of separate środowiska; they will not become koleżanki (colleagues) or refer to each other as ty. The two women appreciate the difference in their status, which will remain clearly defined. Though it is often in the best interest of both parties to establish a personal relationship, this by no means blurs the distinct social hierarchical structure.

In relationships between social unequals, superiors are expected to do "free favors" upon occasion. Carrying out a good deed without a reciprocal return may increase the patron's social standing and prestige.

Barbara benefitted from her mother's relationship with the officer in the officer's club where she works. In return for his good deed of allowing Barbara's cousin a pass for the night, which cost him nothing, the officer will only expect polite appreciation and respect from Barbara's mother. As a client, Barbara's mother cannot really return the favor. When I asked her how she would repay him, she said, "It isn't

necessary . . . Perhaps I will take him flowers or
something."

Out of generosity, people with high social positions can help those with lower status, without expecting reciprocal favors. But, unless a superior is
the only one who can assist in solving a given problem, people generally do not ask their superiors or
elders for help.

Ala did not feel free to ask her former high school
classics teacher for help with an exchange matter.
When Ala needed to *załatwić* curtains, she asked almost everyone in her *środowisko* for leads. But she
did not want to bother the teacher, whom she met
accidentally on the street, with such a concern. The
retired teacher, after chatting, asked Ala if she knew
where toilet paper could be purchased. Ala was happy
to oblige with an answer, even though she did not
ask the teacher, a recognized elder, for leads on curtains.

Family, very close friends, colleagues and "good
acquaintances" are the four types of individuals Poles
invite into their homes for dinner or "parties." Social
position may determine the kind of favor one can
request from another. But the request itself and the
quality of performance may change the relationship
in the direction of less or more social distance. Acquaintances become close friends, and close friends
may become relatives through marriage. Marriage,
family and friendship relationships may move apart
or even break up completely.

During disruptive and uncertain times, such as
those of martial law, people mobilize their support
networks for the exchange of goods, services and
privileges. Pan B's wife obtains meat, coffee and shoes
through private channels. When gasoline becomes
scarce, officially available only with ration cards, Pan
B. turns to a colleague to *załatwić* extra rations. Pan
B. may consciously cultivate a new contact or build
a new network for instrumental purposes in mo-

ments of distress. Yet, even in such times, he relies mainly on existing networks to achieve new purposes. He is skilled in knowing the right person at the right place at the right time.

An atmosphere of crisis encourages people to mobilize existing networks, and also to create new ones. For instance, a particular meat store in Warsaw serves as a social center for retired citizens. Many seniors hire themselves out to stand in line for meat for others who have less time to do so. Their "work" creates a situation in which they meet often and they converse as if they were sitting in a cafe.

Poles entertain to reinforce familial and close friendship ties and establish closer, more personal relationships with work colleagues and acquaintances. They know that most everything is best accomplished on the basis of a personal relationship.

*   *   *

I asked a number of people whom they can truly depend on. People rely on institutions and official organizations only in very limited cases.

Though Barbara is a devout Catholic and steadfastly attends mass each Sunday, she does not meet people at church and does not feel that the Church itself would help her in times of need. "The Church doesn't have this kind of organization," she explained.

In fact, there is no organization in Poland in which Barbara has confidence, which she believes she could really count on.

"If you need help," I pressed, "Isn't there any organization you could depend on?"'

"No, there isn't anything like that," she insisted.

Barbara said she really has faith only in her family. "I know that I can count on them," she insisted.

"The role of the Church" has received considerable attention in the Western media. Yet very few people I talked with felt they could rely on the Church for help. It is true that Grażyna sings in a church choir and Pani Janina takes advantage of relief items distributed by the Church. It is also true that the Church organized a whole system of aid to help internees and their families. It sponsored programs by actors and exhibits by artists, which, in many cases, were veiled protests against martial law or government policies and could not have been put on elsewhere, except illegally and for much smaller audiences.

The Church aids some in political trouble, sponsors cultural activities and provides forums for some to meet. But most people do not depend on the Church for help in times of need and they do not generally meet people there.

One individual commented, "The Church would help me out if I were put in jail, but my *przyjaciele* would help me out first anyway." Another individual, who attends mass only on special occasions told me, "I never tried relying on the Church. I wouldn't go to them. I heard the Church helps people they know, more or less."

Some people received legal assistance and help in solving bureaucratic and material problems from Solidarity when it was a legal organization. Yet, under the circumstances imposed by martial law and beyond, people did not feel they could rely on Solidarity as an organization, just as they did not feel they could rely on the Church. An individual who claimed to be active in underground Solidarity commented, "As an organization, I doubt I can rely on them. I think it is the opposite; they can rely on me. If I were unemployed, networks of friends and acquaintances connected to Solidarity could try to help. Not long ago, I was asked for help by a friend who was looking for a job for someone connected with Solidarity neither I nor my friend had met."

Though the Church and Solidarity are symbolically important to urban Poles, these organizations do not generally sponsor forums or activities that organize people socially. In the absence of organizations that create sharing and trust among people, loyalty to one's family and small circle of close friends is paramount.

In Poland there are few social organizations which people rely on outside of their family. In contrast to the West, where interest groups spring up to meet almost every need, it does not occur to Poles to form such groups. Privatization is so firmly rooted in their lives that public interest groups do not create a rallying point for loyalties. Kin, friends and neighbors fulfill people's material and social needs. People seem to rely on organizations only insofar as they may be useful as networks for special privileges.

One example is membership in the Veterans' Union. A veteran is defined as anyone who was imprisoned in a concentration camp, and/or served in the underground army or resistance, and/or served in the Polish Army in the Soviet Union or Western Europe, and/or served in the state army until 1948. In order to qualify as a veteran, one needs two witnesses. The special legal rights accorded veterans are also extended to their immediate families. The rules for status as a "veteran" keep changing. And the benefits increase. It is no wonder, then, that 40 years after the war, while membership in many official clubs and organizations has steadily declined since 1980, membership in the Veterans' Union has increased from 329,500 in 1970 to 764,200 in 1984, an increase of almost two and one half.

A Polish sociologist described the usual lack of dependency on large social organizations this way:

> A basic feature for Poland, which differentiates Polish society, is that there exists a different level of societal integration. The lowest level is the family and, possibly, the social circle; the highest is "the nation." "Society" identi-

fies with "the nation," and in the middle is a huge social vacuum.

Acquaintances serve as momentary links between a small "island," comprised of family, and, often, close friends and colleagues, and other "islands" of family. Acquaintances form a permanent ad hoc social structure.

Polish family ties have been especially strengthened during the recent years of economic crisis. Before the 1970s and the economic expansion years lead by Edward Gierek, there was talk about the "crisis of the family," and, at the same time, membership in organizations and clubs grew steadily. Though public discussion and conscious public policy on the family had previously been the prerogative of the Church, Gierek embarked on a policy to strengthen family ties and to lessen the Church's hold on the family. But with the economic decline of the late 1970s and early 1980s, the family has strengthened itself. Public discussion on the "crisis of the family" would seem ridiculous in the present context. While no one would speak of the "crisis of the family" now, membership in most formal organizations has declined dramatically since 1980. People have retreated to the ranks of their friends and families.

If families have become islands allocating resources unto themselves, what, if anything, is the Church, the main non-government organization, doing to counter this? According to officials in some Catholic organizations, there is concern about the lack of "integrating structure" between family units, both in rural and urban areas. One church official admitted, "We have too little experience in community life ourselves."

Since the 1970s, however, the Church has attempted to organize small communities in parishes, especially among youth. I attended such a meeting, which reminded me of an American evangelical

Protestant service. The meeting was complete with testimonials about private faith experiences. Participants introduced guests who also shared. To guitar accompaniment, people sang American evangelical songs, translated into Polish.

In the 1980s, this movement towards community has grown. There is currently a move underway in Warsaw to organize parents belonging to particular parishes for regular devotional meetings and cooperation in childcare. It is a small attempt to preclude what church officials see as the "atomization" of society. The project is an experimental one, and with antagonistic church-state relations in mind, one church worker told me, "It's better to simply take action and not to talk about it."

Ala, who lived for extended periods both in New York and Paris but came back to Poland to settle, explained the distinctive importance of the Polish family:

> Family life in Poland is different from the West. Children, young people, adults live with their parents much longer. People marry later. They live with their parents even after marriage. There's not that big sense of turning 18 and running off and being on your own, of "being independent." Family life is very important. Our families are all we have.

4

Who To Believe

In December of 1982, United States Secretary of Defense, Caspar Weinberger, commented that General Jaruzelski was a "Russian in Polish uniform." Shortly thereafter, Jaruzelski announced that cultural contacts with the United States would be terminated and that Americans on cultural and scientific exchanges could be sent home. The evening news aired a forceful government announcement: Poland would institute "sanctions" against the United States. The next morning's newspaper, *Trybuna Ludu (The People's Tribune)*, the main Communist Party daily, was filled with equally harsh anti-American sentiments.

After hearing the news, I was distressed—I wanted to stay in Poland to complete my doctoral research. I went nervously to the American Embassy, anticipating that officials there had already received an official communique from the Polish government regarding the status of foreign researchers. Would we have to leave Poland tomorrow? The cultural affairs officers were sleepless and rattled. But the embassy had received no official word, no clarification whatsoever, of the startling announcement.

With no official explanation of the announcement, several conflicting interpretations surfaced. When I told a professor at the university that the embassy had received no official message, he reasoned that, "Probably they're just trying to sound harsh. There's a 75 percent chance this announcement won't concern you." One friend guessed no action would be taken until after the approaching Christmas; another was sure that if anything happened at all, it would happen very quickly. But nothing happened quickly or in the weeks before Christmas.

I went to the embassy every day to see if there was official news or even unofficial word about the future of cultural exchanges. But still there was no clarification.

In the meantime, everyone continued to speculate. After consulting with well-placed personal contacts, the director of a university institute predicted that future, rather than current, grant-holders would be affected. An engineer I met at a New Year's Eve party had heard from other sources that the announcement was designed to prevent Polish scientists from travelling abroad, not Americans coming to Poland. "It's aimed at members of the intellectual opposition who people look up to," the engineer said.

But a journalist friend told me he thought the announcement was a case of "big cloud, little rain." He advised me not to worry, "They don't announce something if they're going to take action." He was right. Despite the uproar, visas for cultural exchanges remained valid.

My experience shows how Poles construct their own versions of "truth" based on word-of-mouth information and their own readings of the official media. The state-controlled media are seldom taken at face value. They are part of what is elusive in Polish life—a source of speculation and skepticism. People turn to news passed by word of mouth, Western news and the underground press as more reflective of the truth than the "propaganda" of the official media.

Poland has two main levels of information—official and private—and the two frequently contradict each other. Every day, Poles are informed through the morning newspaper and evening television that Poland's economy is "continually developing." Yet, every day, they may have to stand in lines to put food on the evening dinner table, fight the crowds and, if they want better-quality goods, frequent store after store in search of them. Poles are well aware that they may have to wait years to obtain an apartment or to get the plumbing fixed and months to buy a new coat or pair of shoes. There is a wide discrepancy between people's daily experiences and the picture of those same realities presented by much of the daily mass media.

THROUGH THE OFFICIAL LOOKING GLASS

Poles find the predictable, official form of the news—aired on television and printed in many newspapers—difficult to take seriously. Acquaintances viewed with amusement a special television news program aired in the spring of 1982 about how life had improved since the imposition of martial law. To a background of dramatic, turbulent music, the commentator described Solidarity's disruptive influence on society. Then Chopin's calm music played as the television pictured abundant goods in stores— martial law had replaced chaos with tranquility.

Poles whose daily lives were in a state of upheaval could not help but be amused by official publications that presented "evidence" of the stable situation in the country. A 1984 article in the Party newspaper *Trybuna Ludu* reads:

> The number of passengers LOT Polish airlines carried in 1984 is close to the number carried before the crisis, which shows that life in Poland is returning to normal.

Friends were similarly entertained by a radio program on "free Saturdays" (non-working Saturdays).

The government program tried to convince listeners that free Saturdays are not in their best interest. "If something goes wrong in your apartment on a free Saturday," the speaker informed listeners, "you won't be able to find anyone to fix it."

Both domestic and international news are often infused with official ideology and delivered dogmatically. News reports cover such politically sensitive subjects as demonstrations and consumer issues. But they are frequently harassing in tone and unclear.

Official news reports are often worded in a style which assumes unquestionable givens. Journalists and officials frequently use certain phrases such as "as it is known." For instance, "as it is known" was sufficient evidence in official news accounts to substantiate that economic depression in Poland was caused only by Solidarity strikes and American sanctions imposed after martial law, and bore no relation to poor economic planning of the 1970s. "As it is known" implies that everyone knows and accepts as truth that which "is known." Those using this construction need not specify who *everyone* is.

A 1983 article in the official *Dziennik Bałtycki (The Daily Baltic)* printed in Gdańsk, the former Solidarity center, reads:

> The forthcoming papal visit is a sign and proof of advancing normalization in this country. Precisely for that reason, the visit is not much to the liking of the internal opposition and external enemies. By inciting public unrest, they try to prevent the visit from taking place and to prove to the world that Poland is an internally torn and divided country.
>
> By creating disturbances, they can hide their own anxieties and their temptations to change the existing state of affairs.
>
> The aforementioned attempts to arouse tension, which Western radio stations try to compare to national insurgencies, show that not everyone has Poland's best interests at heart, and that the state, being the institution responsible for the fate of society, must make these people

aware of the difference between good and evil. If necessary, the state must resort to force, even if this is painful for undisciplined individuals. When one takes to the streets to do some shouting at the foot of a monument, he should bear this in mind.

The future of the country will not be discussed in the streets, at a monument or with the help of stones and verbal abuse.

The predictably rote style of the media led one friend to remark, "You can't listen to the propaganda even when its true."

The official media are the butt of numerous cynical jokes. A Warsaw theater production I attended featured these lines:

Man 1: My wife died from a fit of laughter.
Man 2: How?
Man 1: From watching the news.
The audience roared.

The official media are censored under an elaborate system directed by the Main Office for the Control of Press, Publications and Public Performances, which, informally, is responsible to the Press Department of the Communist Party's Central Committee. This office has bureaus located throughout the country that oversee all media. The press, television, radio, books, theater, film, concerts, festivals, and exhibitions are subject to censorship, as are stamps, nonstandard wedding invitations, match boxes and cigarette packs. The government also controls rations of paper and the printing and distribution of all print media. Since censorship guidelines are themselves censored, it is difficult to know what is off-limits at any given time.

With the birth and legalization of Solidarity, new information and criticism appeared in the official press that could not have been printed previously. Even the most official of state-controlled newspapers, such as *Trybuna Ludu*, began printing news articles and editorials criticizing the leadership and its policies. Radio and television programming opened up, but television news remained carefully censored. In April of 1981, Solidarity finally won the concession to print its own weekly newspaper. *Tygodnik Solidarność (Solidarity Weekly)* enjoyed a wide readership.

With the declaration of martial law in December of 1981, Solidarity was outlawed and its publications were banned. The printing of all formerly legal newspapers, except for two official papers—*Trybuna Ludu* and *Żołnierz Wolności (Soldier of Freedom)*, daily paper of the Polish People's Army—was temporarily halted. Many journalists did not pass required "verification" to prove their loyalty to the government or left the profession voluntarily. Printing of most publications has since resumed, but under strict censorship. Yet in 1983, a law was passed to regulate the activities of censorship offices. Now an author or editor has the official right to appeal a censorship decision to a higher office. An editor can show that the censor omitted something in a book or article by inserting [----] in place of what was deleted.

Censorship guidelines vary with the political climate. In the 1970s the media's "propaganda of success" painted a positive picture of society, even though, by the middle of the decade, it was apparent that the "economic miracle" would not be fulfilled. In the 1980s, despite the crackdown of martial law, the media disclosed more true information on the country's economy. The situation is uneven. A Polish philosopher told me that in the 1970s the government allowed certain underground activities not permitted now, "Yet some of my articles rejected by censors in the 1970s now appear in *Polityka!*"

Though the government allows more open discussion of economic problems now than in the 1970s, the source of those problems is a touchier issue. It is advisable in the media to blame economic decline on Western sanctions and creditors rather than attribute deterioration to Polish economic decision makers or to "the system."

The need for elaborate censorship rules attests to the fact that those working in the media, even those with 40 years of postwar training, cannot be tagged government loyalists or be expected to toe official lines. Censors themselves are better characterized as bureaucrats than "believers."

Most rules in Poland give way to maneuver and manipulation, and censorship is no exception. Producers, censors, and supervising government organs and Party officials all vie for their own interests. Censorship depends not only on the times but also on the connections and political clout of individual editors and producers during those times.

Circulation size is decisive in a censor's evaluation. Some bits of news are not permitted at all; others are allowed but must be presented in a stated way; still others are permissible only in specific publications or for particular audiences. In general, the more limited the audience, the more criticism is allowed. Socio-political weeklies are allowed more latitude than dailies, but less than small-circulation journals. Recent sociology journals carry articles on the Solidarity and martial law periods, addressing issues relating to these periods with candid criticism.

Even seasoned authors and editors cannot be certain from one day to the next what will pass the censors. The censorship process is most uncertain for writers. Because writers are accustomed to conveying ideas through euphemism, censors can be overly cautious. A poet who used the word *wrona* in a stanza was dumbstruck to learn that the stanza had been censored. *Wrona* means "crow" but was also an acronym for the martial law government. The censor judged that the poet was criticizing martial law by his reference to crow.

While censorship works to create a particular picture of Poland and the world, independent viewpoints frequently appear. The media go far beyond the official daily publications, two television channels and four radio stations that serve as an arm of the ruling elite. Some intellectual weeklies furnish more autonomous commentary and analyses of events.

Polityka, Życie Gospodarcze (Economic Life), and *Przegląd Techniczny* (Technical Review) are widely circulated weekly newspapers that cover political, economic and social affairs. Though censored, *Życie Gospodarcze*, the Polish equivalent of *The Wall Street Journal*, often prints reliable articles on the economic situation. *Przegląd Techniczny* reports on issues pertaining to technology and industry. *Polityka* publishes credible reports and commentary on current events.

The Catholic Church also commands an extensive press, though it has no access to radio and television, except for weekly masses. According to some Catholic sources, there are a total of 105 Catholic periodicals in Poland—either direct arms of the Church or merely edited and censored by the Church. Church publications include papers with wide appeal and circulation, newsletters printed by individual dioceses, quarterly scholarly magazines published by the Catholic University of Lublin and periodicals produced by the Catholic Intelligentsia Club, such as the independent monthly *Więź (Bond)*. Published by the Catholic group *Znak*, the weekly *Tygodnik Powszechny (Universal Weekly)*, and the monthly *Znak* (Sign) cater to religious and nonreligious alike. *Tygodnik Powszechny* prints "The Week in Review," a widely-read column which treats critically government policies and measures.

Most censorship in Poland is self-censorship. Constantly mindful of the restrictions imposed by formal institutions, most editors and authors censor themselves. Though, during the Solidarity period, people began to unlearn the self-censorship they were masters of, the climate of fear, caution and conformity returned with the imposition of martial law.

More or less aware of the parameters of what is acceptable, writers, producers, and editors carefully test the boundaries of acceptability. A writer and a censor may discuss an article and arrive at a compromise, obscuring or omitting that which may not be overtly stated. An acquaintance of mine, a social scientist, wrote an article for *Życie Gospodarcze* on prospects for economic reform in Poland. In his lengthy article he concluded that the economic system could not be reformed because it is so closely tied to the political system. The censor could not allow this to pass his authority. Together, the censor and the writer worked out wording which modified the unacceptably explicit statement but left nuances of the same idea untouched. The article was published.

Sometimes the official media print private information in a veiled form that everyone can see through. Advertisements in *Życie Warszawy*, a popular Warsaw daily, pass on hidden messages, unintelligible to foreigners but immediately understood by Poles. "Returned from abroad, looking for an apartment," indicates that the advertiser has been in the West and earned enough dollars to buy or rent an apartment. "Apartments for rent to foreigners" means that the landlord will rent the apartment only for hard currency. Likewise, newspaper advertisements to buy and sell *bony* (legal dollar substitutes) are usually disguised notices for black market trade in dollars.

Outside news, imported or reprinted in the Polish press, is to some extent available in Poland. The weekly magazine *Forum* is composed entirely of reprinted articles, translated into Polish, which appeared originally in foreign presses. In a 1984 issue of *Forum*, I read an interview with former President Jimmy Carter from *Time*, an article on the nuclear arms race from *The New York Times* and a talk with the President of Iraq, Sadam Husajn, from *Stern*. Other issues featured "A Small Encyclopedia of the

Common Market," reprinted from *The Economist*, a cartoon from the *Bulletin of the Atomic Scientists* and Art Buchwald's column. Though the articles selected for publication in *Forum* generally have been screened to weed out those which might criticize or challenge the official ideology of Poland, the Soviet Union and other Soviet-bloc countries, *Forum* nevertheless provides its readers access in their own language to issues and viewpoints articulated in the world press.

Demand for *Forum*, *Polityka* and *Życie Gospodarcze* outweighs the usual supply, and they are frequently available only on the day of the weekly delivery. Sometimes people obtain them through special arrangements with the women who work in the newsstands.

The foreign press, imported to Poland, is not widely available in original form but can be found. It is impossible to buy *The New York Times*, *Le Monde* or *Die Zeit* at state newspaper stands, yet there are some officially-sanctioned ways of obtaining the Western press. Anyone can frequent *International Press and Book Clubs*, state libraries located in major cities in Poland. There, one can read the world press, including a limited selection of Western magazines and newspapers. Papers containing "anti-Polish" articles, however, generally do not make it to the shelves.

Most of the Polish news, aired on television and radio and printed in official dailies, is routine and predictable. Poles spend a lifetime training themselves to see through its form and content. In reading between the lines, people try to evaluate the purpose for which an event is deemed newsworthy and construe from that what may actually be going on. Sometimes it is easy to interpret the news. For instance, people joked that they knew where to go to demonstrate because broadcasts advised them to "Avoid the Old Town square at 4:00 P.M. today."

Though Poles treat what their media tell them with

great skepticism, the media nevertheless have a definite and powerful effect. Many people tend to automatically believe the opposite of whatever they hear on television or read in the newspapers. A Polish physicist working as a visiting scholar in the United States was shocked when a white South African confirmed that racial conflict actually existed in his country. Apartheid, she had reasoned, was an invention of the Polish mass media.

THE GRAPEVINE

Many Poles more readily accept private information, conveyed through word of mouth and unofficial or foreign media, than government news sources. Private news has many and varied sources—from personal experiences and speculation to underground tracts and Western news, including broadcasts of Radio Free Europe, Voice of America and the British Broadcasting Corporation (BBC).

One source of private news—though less important in daily life than word-of-mouth information—is the underground press. It is a conduit of privately shared information and often a source of the grapevine reports that are the Polish alternative to state censorship. The postwar underground press took shape as intellectual opposition groups founded a series of underground publications in the latter part of the 1970s. They were in reaction to Gierek's "propaganda of success."

The labor unrest of 1976 provided the immediate impetus for the underground press. In June of 1976 a rise in meat prices triggered workers' strikes and demonstrations throughout Poland. Though the government was forced to rescind the price hikes immediately, the government initially arrested hundreds of workers, some of whom they eventually sentenced.

In September of 1976 a group of intellectuals formed KOR, an acronym for Committee for the Defense of Workers, in the aftermath of the June arrests. KOR published *Komunikat (Communique)*, which described KOR's activities in supplying legal and financial assistance to imprisoned workers and their families, and reported on subsequent arrests, detentions and trials.

Another KOR publication, *Biuletyn Informacyjny (Bulletin of Information)*, dealt with repression, the economy, domestic issues such as the Pope's 1979 trip to Poland, and foreign policy concerns such as the SALT treaty negotiations. 1979 issues of *Biuletyn Informacyjny* included articles by Professor Edward Lipiński, widely recognized as grandfather of the Polish opposition, and Adam Michnik and Jacek Kuron, now famous opposition leaders. In 1979, KOR workers distributed 5,000 to 7,000 copies of the publication, each one filled with some 70 light brown, coarse pages, throughout Poland.

Soon after the founding of KOR, other opposition groups, sometimes at odds with KOR, sprung up. By 1978 various underground organizations published some 20 papers. The number of copies printed was limited, but many people read each one.

The legalization of Solidarity created the atmosphere and conditions for the further development of the underground press. Political diversification within the opposition brought about a press explosion. But martial law was imposed only one and a half years later. Many Solidarity leaders were interned, and Solidarity was largely disarmed. Yet underground bulletins appeared almost overnight, and the illegal press has since grown.

Poland's underground culture has received much attention from the West. It cannot be denied that, in its content, underground culture rivals officially blessed culture; and underground media is a counterpoint to official media. But the same cannot be claimed for the extent of the underground culture or its impact on everyday life.

It would have been nearly impossible to live in Poland without witnessing some of the varied forms of underground expression—illegal newspapers, books, exhibitions, educational courses, cabarets and theaters. Once I happened upon underground literature lying visibly on the table of a university classroom. In the early months of martial law, some students defiantly wore Solidarity buttons; others wore miniature red electrical resistors, a symbol of resistance to martial law; and when the authorities caught on to that, still other symbols appeared.

A University professor sipped tea in the cafe of Warsaw's *Europejski* hotel, wearing a symbolic resistance button his wife had made for him. A man approached him and asked what the button meant. Suspecting the inquirer of being a secret police agent, the professor was quick to outsmart him. "Oh this," the professor calmly replied, "Don't you know what this is? It's a new form of Russian art!"

Spokespeople for the underground claim that "underground leaflets can be found in practically every Polish home." This is disputable. Yet, without solicitation on my part, people were keen to show me weekly underground tracts and books, including those by Nobel Prize winning poet, Czesław Miłosz, and by Tadeusz Konwicki, a prominent Polish writer, all hot off underground presses. They also showed me books by Western authors and by Russian and East European dissidents, translated into Polish from the original languages. With reverence, as if handling precious family photographs, they were eager to display the trappings of martial law: photographs of crowds holding up fingers in "V" signs, of Lech Wałęsa with the Pope, of demonstrations and arrests and even of political prisoners in deten-

tion. More recently, sermons by the Father Jerzy Popiełuszko, the priest murdered by agents of the security police, have become popular underground fare.

Distributing leaflets on the street is unheard of—
one has to know from whom to obtain them. Since
any form of distribution is illegal and potentially
dangerous, people tend to pass them on only to
trusted friends, family members and colleagues.

Polish underground culture is a far cry from Soviet
underground *samizdat*, in which several thousand
intellectuals produce primitive-quality manuscripts by
hand on their typewriters. In Poland, there is a huge
market for underground culture and its production
entails a widespread, sophisticated system. Underground presses thrive despite the vigilance of authorities, sporadic paper shortages and state control
of printing and duplicating equipment. Hundreds of
thousands of books, millions of copies of newspapers and thousands of cassettes containing songs,
lectures and cabarets are distributed annually. The
production of underground culture follows many of
the rules of an independent market mechanism: prices
are regulated according to production cost and there
is some competition between publishing houses.

In 1984, according to some underground sources,
approximately 500 books and pamphlets were printed
illegally, almost as many as are produced annually
by two of the largest official publishing houses. An
underground activist described how an underground book is produced:

> The first printing for an average book in a respectable
> underground publishing house is about 5,000 copies. A
> 200-page book requires about 500 packages of paper which
> contain 500 pieces each. Five hundred packages is a small
> truck load of paper.
>   Paper is generally obtained *na lewo*, for in such quan-
> tities it is impossible to buy it in a store. This is no easy
> feat. The authorities reviewed enterprises that ordered
> substantial quantities of paper and one of them turned out

to be a front for an underground organization. Delivery trucks had come regularly to collect paper supplies, and representatives had had appropriate documents in hand, but this firm—which had ordered the most paper—existed only on paper!

Obtaining paper is only the first problem. Printing is generally carried out in private homes or *na lewo* in state enterprises. Printing materials and equipment must be obtained. People and vehicles to distribute them for sale must be arranged. Hundreds of people are involved in this process, supported by underground coffers filled through extensive, secret collection networks.

Everyone is paid—writers, editors, and technical workers. Writers and editors earn about as much (or slightly better) salaries than they would in comparable official positions. The general rule is, the higher the risk of arrest and prosecution, the higher the salary. Thus printers earn more for their time than writers and editors.

Western observers often wonder why underground culture cannot be eradicated or significantly reduced by authorities. One compelling reason is that many people without ideological motivation for their activities are involved in underground operations: the clerk who sells paper *na lewo;* the printer who earns more money working for Solidarity than he would for the state; and the man who rents his villa for the exorbitant price of 100,000 złoty monthly, purposely not asking any questions about what he knows must be an illegal operation.

As one underground spokesman put it: "Even if they would arrest Lech Wałęsa and Zbigniew Bujak [underground leader in hiding] and a thousand Polish activists, the show would go on—you'll always find people who want to earn money. Idealism need not contradict materialism—that is the biggest invention of the Polish opposition."

A 1984 article in *Trybuna Ludu* goes so far as to acknowledge the existence of the clandestine press and its continued growth. The government publication then counters with the far-fetched claim that underground newspapers were not meant for use within Poland and concludes with a sentence of circular non-logic.

> Some experts belonging to the political opposition claim that underground circulation of bulletins and other publications now exceeds the number present in 1980 and 1981. Although this might be true, a number of these publications have very small circulation and are intended for use abroad rather than within the country. Hence, it is not true to claim that these publications were censored, since they were never submitted for publication.

So disbelieving are Poles of their own official media that they tend to accept uncritically any word from the West. They listen to broadcasts of the BBC, Radio Free Europe, and Voice of America—sporadically jammed by the government—for the latest political news, coverage of demonstrations and unrest. At private gatherings during times of upheaval, people stop drinking and talking to listen attentively to foreign radio reports, often comparing the news presented in all three and tuning in to both Polish and English language broadcasts. According to a 1983 survey conducted by the government's Center for Public Opinion and Broadcasting Research, 30 percent of the adult population acknowledged that they listen to foreign radio broadcasts.

What Radio Free Europe or BBC said about a topic is circulated by word of mouth. Western news magazines are much more difficult to gain access to than radio broadcasts, and a more elite group has access to them, yet issues of *Time, Newsweek, Der Spiegel* and *Le Monde,* as well as what people report to have been in them, are circulated through informal networks. Because Western information is prized and believed over Polish media, Western media has a considerable impact on Polish views.

Polish authorities know the impact of Western news and try to use it to their own advantage in their re-

ports. A 1985 article in *Rzeczpospolita (Republic)* reports on General Jaruzelski's trip to the United States
for a United Nations session:

> Early in the afternoon Premier Jaruzelski met with the
> management of *Time* Inc., whose publications have a total
> circulation of 16 million. The weekly *Time*, one of the most
> serious periodicals in the world, published an interview
> with the General Secretary of the Communist Party of the
> Soviet Union, Mikhail Gorbachev, a few weeks ago.
>
> Jaruzelski talked with the management of *Time* Inc., of
> which Henry Grunwald is head. It should be recalled here
> that Grunwald visited Poland, together with a group of
> American businessmen in October 1981, and was received
> on that occasion by Premier Jaruzelski.

The message conveyed in the article is that Jaruzelski must be an important, respectable person because Henry Grunwald and *Time* wanted to meet with
him.

Poles are easily persuaded that "an enemy of my
enemy is my friend." Staunchly anti-Soviet and an-
ticommunist, many Poles see the United States as
savior. Despite counter-productive and damaging
economic effects to the Polish economy, many Poles
supported President Reagan's martial law sanctions
against Poland, since they saw Reagan as firmly anti-
Soviet. Though Pentagon strategies for "limited nuclear war" would destroy Poland first, Poles seem to
be largely unconcerned about this possibility.

A friend related his observation: "How do Poles
imagine that American Pershing rockets fly over Poland? In a zigzag course. They avoid Poles, but hit
Communists!" Indeed the threat of nuclear catastrophe is largely dismissed as anti-American propaganda disseminated by the Polish mass media.

Uncritical acceptance of Western news is the cor-
ollary of Poles' almost complete lack of faith in their
media. Western media and underground presses
supply information, usually of a political nature,
which, in the official media, is viewed with skepti-

cism. Alternative news sources supplement the grapevine, which is the lifeblood of everyday life. News from Western press or special bulletins provide the basis of much word-of-mouth information.

Well-placed officials and information are also central sources for the grapevine. Though ostensibly "For Internal Circulation Only," I stumbled onto a copy of *Biuletyn Specjalny (Special Bulletin)* distributed to about 1,000 highly-placed media and government officials. In contrast to the narrow and predictable nature of the official media, *Biuletyn Specjalny* is informative and objective, covers internationally newsworthy items and summarizes articles from respected international sources such as the *Washington Post*, Associated Press and Reuters. *Biuletyn Nasłuchów (The Monitoring Bulletin)* is another limited-circulation journal intended for the highest officials. It contains texts of foreign Polish language radio broadcasts including BBC, Radio Free Europe and Voice of America. News contained in such bulletins often goes beyond its intended recipients, becoming sources of grapevine information.

*   *   *

The English language lacks terms that accurately describe information passed on by word of mouth. This is not mere "rumor," which usually refers to untruths, or "gossip," which means idle or frivolous chatter. In Poland access to private information channels is the key to success and even survival.

Everyone—from the highest official to the cleaning woman employed in public restrooms (who collects złoty from clients)—relies on the grapevine. An acquaintance, a well-known actor, was notified, not by the Ministry of Culture, but by chance, that he had received a prestigious international acting award. "I only found out about it this morning when a friend mentioned he read it in the newspaper," the actor told me. Everything from everyday survival concerns to major political and social events provides fuel for the grapevine. In the company of trusted individuals, gossip and the swapping of information are more than interesting pastimes—they are vital to managing life.

In dinner conversation, social gatherings, work and professional meetings, as well as in buses and lines, people swap news. Information is the most basic and valuable exchange commodity in Poland, for, without knowing who, how and where, it is not possible to *załatwić* anything. Many commodities are scarce in Poland, but, ordinarily, correct information is one of the hardest to come by. People keep tabs on who among their friends and acquaintances can help who to do what. Those who are most successful in economic, political and social arenas are generally people who can probe and retain information, find out who is who and connect themselves to particularly adept, well-placed individuals in information networks.

People collect and store information for future reference and use, setting up a system of trade-offs and favors. Except for employees, no Poles are allowed to enter the stores for Western diplomats in the commissaries of Western embassies, yet several acquaintances of mine were able to list exactly what goods could be obtained in various stores. The most successful people in Poland are data banks of information, people who know or can learn for themselves, their families and other "insiders."

Unofficial information is often needed in dealing with formal structures and bureaucracies. Obtaining reliable information from the office charged with providing it is sometimes nearly impossible. Public offices are often not marked, and they usually provide no signs on how to proceed once one has discovered the correct location. It is private information, either from outside or inside the bureaucracy, which facilitates, or even makes possible, the completion of a task.

Chasing information was inevitably part of my daily routine. In order to get an international student identification card, I was sent from one office to another, to a third, which sent me back to the first. At the university I was often unable to locate rooms in which seminars were ostensibly to be held. Not even those in charge of the building or of scheduling could give me what I would consider to be correct, reliable information. As one secretary at the university put it, "In the East, information is not distributed directly."

I received notice of a gift arrival from Ariton, a company that delivers parcels to Poland. With the aid of a detailed map drawn by a friend and information from half a dozen passersby, I finally found the unmarked, dimly lit, smoke-filled Ariton office in the back of a warehouse. Here were 70 to 80 people crowded into a small room. Such rarities as Kelloggs Corn Flakes, Vienna coffee, Juicy Fruit gum, Bic razor blades, cooked ham, mayonnaise and laundry detergent were displayed behind locked glass cabinets.

No official information or instructions were posted, and it was impossible to see even the clerks at the front of the room. I relied on information from people in the room to learn that I would need to stand in three separate lines and to locate the first line I would stand in. Several hours into the process, new arrivals asked me the same questions I had asked earlier. The only alternative required pushing one's way through the resentful crowd to ask the clerks, who were tremendously irritated at having to answer the same questions hundreds of times every day. It was only the private exchange of information that allowed the office to function at all.

I had received the equivalent of a $40 gift certificate, and, after a long wait in line, was handed a list of goods to choose from, with instructions to take my completed list to yet another clerk. It was only back in line, talking with other customers, that I found out that over half of the goods on the official list were unavailable, while some not mentioned were actually in stock. With the help of this shared, unofficial information, customers successfully filled out request slips. I passed the information on to newcomers.

Word-of-mouth information facilitates the functioning of bureaucracies. Bureaucrats expect that consumers have access to such information. In fact, bureaucrats often become irritated if a customer comes to them having ignored informal channels, because this makes their work more difficult.

Informal information is necessary not only for consumers but also for those whose jobs are tied to the official bureaucracy or government apparatus. The successful execution of many jobs and functions depends in large measure on the grapevine.

Information unofficially circulated is accorded more credibility than official sources, resulting in a body of shared private knowledge. The locations of many commonplace black market activities are well-known. The street corners in Warsaw on which alcohol can be bought and sold illegally are common knowledge. Everyone knows of their existence, but no one would admit it in public.

The informal exchange of information is an established system, and people base everyday decisions— such as where to get *na lewo* gas rations—on information delivered via the grapevine. The almost continual reports that "next month's ration cards will include no meat" send people desperately looking for ways to *załatwić* meat. In other instances, news passed by word of mouth is the basis for landmark life decisions such as when and where to emigrate.

Rumors abound. During the first tense months of martial law, I heard numerous reports from discern-

ing intellectuals, who were convinced they were repeating factual information. These included stories
that Soviet troops had invaded Poland, that a natu-
ral catastrophe had occurred in Moscow and no one
could enter or leave the city and that Polish political
prisoners had been sent to the Soviet Union for in-
definite internment. None of the reports turned out
to be true.

Word-of-mouth reports and private predictions
constantly circulated during martial law and continue to circulate. Since General Jaruzelski imposed
martial law in December of 1981, there have been
reports that he was about to lose power and that the
Soviets and the Party apparatchiks wanted to get
rid of him. Well-connected sources report him to be
"extremely nervous" about both the opposition and
his position with the Soviets. Yet Jaruzelski remains
in power.

Speculation about impending war is endless. The
grapevine carried news of supposedly secret negotiations between General Jaruzelski's government and
the underground, which I learned of from a participant. But I was unable to verify frequent word-of-
mouth reports about negotiations between the Church
and the government. I heard news of an impending
amnesty for political prisoners five months before it
was declared in July of 1982.

Just as one is constantly privy to word-of-mouth
news, one is often quizzed for information. I travelled with a Polish friend to visit her aunt and uncle
in Toruń. When we arrived after a long and tiring
train ride, our hosts' first questions were, "What
happened in Warsaw in the beginning of May, during the demonstrations, specifically, May the third?
What did you hear about what happened in Torun?
Did you hear of the severe punishment authorities
meted out to students for their part in demonstrations? Coed dormitories are now segregated!" My
travel companion was, for her part, eager to learn

what had happened in Torun on May 3rd. "Is it true that . . ." she began.

During those uneasy times, the conversation always seemed to begin with an exchange of information about the latest unrest and political speculation. Whenever I travelled outside Warsaw to visit friends in other towns and cities, I was asked, "what *really* happened" in Warsaw on a given day of political unrest? And, of course, I was informed without even asking, what *really* happened on the same day in the part of Poland I was visiting.

My responses to questions about "America" and "the West" travelled beyond the people who asked them. One of the most important ways of gaining exposure to the West for Poles who have not travelled there is through Western friends. Poles welcome Western friends warmly and with unabated curiosity, quizzing them about the latest car models, current salaries for doctors or dentists and the most recent films and novels. I was embarrassed on several occasions when I could not relate to my eager listeners just who had starred in a given film or remember the details of the plot of a recent novel.

In 1985, after the AIDS epidemic in the West had received much attention in the Polish media, many were curious for detailed information about it and expected me to tell them more. Foreigners are expected to contribute to the grapevine.

The rapidity with which grapevine news travels and the long distances it covers are astounding. In the spring of 1984, friends told me they had heard that Elton John had agreed to perform in Poland, but only on the condition that he would be able to meet Lech Wałęsa. Later, I was told by still other friends that John had personally delivered tickets for his concert to the Wałęsa residence and that the Wałęsa family had attended the performance. Neither I nor the people who repeated the news to me are in contact with Wałęsa or his circle of confidants. The official media made no mention of the event. This information—which was later verified in Western press reports and by John—was passed on almost overnight, solely through private networks, from Gdańsk to Warsaw, where I lived, and probably to every city, town and village with inhabitants who cared about such news.

Likewise, everyone knew when, during martial law, an underground Solidarity faction operated a clandestine radio station for several months. The radio frequency and precise air time were circulated by word of mouth. Because police were so efficient in detecting the clandestine broadcasting station, the broadcasts often lasted only for a few minutes before they arrived. Yet people waited by their radios.

The lack of verifiable official information, the slanted nature of the daily media and the unstable political climate all contribute to the central role of informally shared information. Grapevine reports that those arrested during the explosive and chaotic May 3rd demonstration of 1982 would receive prison sentences of several years, as well as a beating, led many mothers to despair. Later word that those arrested would be released after paying a fine—which turned out to be the case in most instances—gave the same mothers some hope. In a situation in which there is rarely a "bottom line," people tend to believe what they hear from sources who themselves may have shaky access to information.

Poles piece together, often haphazardly, accounts and conjecture from various sources. During martial law, Pani R. read in *Trybuna Ludu* that an East German delegation was in town. This reminded her of something that had puzzled her since the previous afternoon: why were all the troops in the city center when there were no scheduled demonstrations or apparent unrest at that time? She thought awhile, then explained confidently, "The government is showing the East Germans we have *Ordnung* in Poland." People discern from whatever sources are available what is actually going on, lending more credence to some than to others. The resulting picture is usually partial—and there is rarely a "final word."

New residential complex far away from city center. Tens of thousands inhabit these gray apartment blocks. The building in the foreground houses a disco, a laundry and a market—the only facilities for social life in the entire complex.

Three generations in one small room: on one side of the wardrobe, grandmother and granddaughter; on the other side of it, the "apartment" of the child's parents. Household articles and personal possessions are stored in and on top of the wardrobe.

Legal private market in Warsaw. Here you can find everything—from oranges and bananas to exotic fruits such as kiwi, mangos and avocados—all unavailable in state stores. Prices are calculated for foreigners: a kilogram of oranges costs one-tenth of the average Polish monthly salary.

A private fisherman pulling fish out of his net.

State store: Polish consumers buy goods at prices set by the government. Fish is being sold from the back of a truck.

Preparation for the Christmas holidays: a line for meat.

To have or not to have: Pewex, a chain of state-owned shops where goods—mostly imported—are sold for hard currency only.

International Press and Book Club—state libraries where one can read the world press. During the period of martial law, most Western newspapers and magazines did not appear on the shelves here.

A lucrative enterprise: "Chmielna Street Band" has a monopoly on street folk music and plays on the sidewalk for "fat" tips.

Honor guard at the Tomb of the Unknown Soldier in Warsaw: the young generation and the past (upper left).

In Warsaw's Old Town, *koleżanki* (girlfriends) from secondary school walk home (lower left).

A beggar on the street: a rare occurrence.

Warsaw's Old Town: a monument to the victims of the Warsaw uprising of 1944.

Cross with flowers decorated with nationalistic symbols: underground leaflets, Solidarity signs, longstanding political declarations and Catholic emblems.

Martial law: a cross on the street. People brought fresh flowers each day as a symbol of protest and hope (upper left).

On the sidewalk, a symbolic "grave" in memory of Father Popiełuszko, the priest brutally murdered by officers of the secret police in 1984 (above right).

The funeral of Father Popiełuszko.

Army of the dead: graves of soldiers who died in the Warsaw uprising of 1944.

Army of the living: village girls.

5

The
Art of
Adjustment

July 3rd, 1983, the day I left Poland for an extended trip to the United States, was a trying day. At the airport I said final good-bys to friends, who encouraged me to "come back to Poland soon." After going to the airline ticket counter to confirm my flight, I waited in line for the first passport and visa control. The controller talked at length on the telephone in a closed-in glass booth, and I began to be suspicious. Finally, he directed me to go to the next checkpoint. I took my luggage to one of the long, low tables where several men—customs officers— were checking the luggage of other passengers. Friends had advised me always to go to a man in customs, but no male customs official would approach me; they seemed automatically to go to other passengers. Finally, a woman with short, bleached-blonde hair appeared from nowhere. I had not seen her checking other passengers. Official and businesslike, she asked for my passport and asked me several questions: Was I going on vacation to the States? What was the purpose of my trip? How much Polish currency did I have with me? How many dollars?

The woman went through my wallet thoroughly. She took a long time, searching everything. Finding a little more Polish currency than I had declared, she loudly and accusingly announced, "You have 1,200 złoty, not 900. You said you had only 900."

After searching my purse, the woman turned to my luggage. I had three big suitcases and a guitar. She began with one of the suitcases, taking everything out and thoroughly examining each item. After 15 minutes had passed and she was still searching through the first piece of luggage, I became impatient. Most of the other passengers had already cleared customs and boarded the plane. We were nearing departure time. I began to ask her politely, "Am I going to make it to the plane?"

She examined the next piece of luggage thoroughly, taking each of the numerous records I had bought out of its cover and looking inside. I became more nervous about departure time. I had few papers with me, and she scrutinized each one. Finally, she called over an assistant to help her with the search. I realized they were intent on checking every single thing. Shoes, clothes, the pages of music books and the inside of my guitar—nothing was spared inspection.

Finally, it seemed they had finished the search. Apparently not having found anything questionable, the woman in charge motioned for the baggage man and put my luggage on the conveyor belt bound for the aircraft.

But the woman did not indicate that I could go. Instead, she hastily led me to a tiny room near the exit to the aircraft. Something was definitely amiss. The official said, "According to Polish law, it is legal to search one personally." I knew what was coming: a strip-search or interrogation session of some kind. Were there concealed cameras? I had nothing to hide, but the situation seemed precarious. I was ordered to take off my jacket, then my dress, then my shoes. As I was shedding clothes, the blonde woman watched me, and the assistant checked the garments. Perhaps I had secret documents sewn into a lining. Though I had no clear idea of what, if anything, they were looking for, I began to feel as though I had done something wrong. I could tell that the search was going to be thorough.

I no longer asked if I would make the plane. "What's this?" questioned the assistant, holding a cassette tape in her hand. She had found a cassette Ala had taped for me and given to me at the airport, simply because she had not had time to deliver it earlier. I became chilled with fear. I felt guilty. Ala had recorded a tape of Russian folk songs for me. Because of the shortage of tapes, she had used a cassette which had formerly contained Solidarity protest songs that an acquaintance had recorded for her. Ala had sworn that the Russian tunes completely covered up the Solidarity songs, but what if she had failed to erase bits of it? The officials would think I was trying to carry subversive material out of Poland. Still, Ala had erased it—the police would hear only innocuous songs if they listened to it.

I mustered my nerve and said confidently, "Those are Russian songs. I am a singer." The customs officials looked at me, unconvinced. Let them check it, I thought. They'll be disappointed to hear tunes. "Please play the tape," I challenged, even more forcefully. The blonde woman hastily examined the tape and handed it back to me.

Finally, the officials were satisfied. They had found nothing suspicious. They told me I could get dressed. I exited the tiny room to find the lobby deserted. I was nervous, frantic to catch my plane. The women were finished with me, but there was yet one more control point. Next to the exit of the plane stood a man in army uniform. My carry-on luggage had to go through a metal detector. I was so upset at that point I practically threw my luggage at him and told him to do with it what he wanted. Taken aback, he smiled and said, "What's wrong? Calm down."

I was the last person to board the plane, a Polish flight bound for Toronto. I felt as though I had done something wrong; I felt people knew I had been strip-searched; I felt singled out, guilty and stained. The feelings were with me even after several drinks and several days of rest back in the United States. For the next few weeks I tried to assign interpretations to everything that had gone on that morning in the airport from the time I walked in to my arrival in Canada. Was I given "special treatment" because I appeared excited and nervous? Or was there a special order from above to search me thoroughly? If so, why? Was I particularly suspicious in the eyes of police authorities? Or was it because I had miscounted my Polish currency? Had I given a suspicious answer to the question, "Are you going on vacation?" Why me? Would I be strip-searched when I returned to Poland? My questions and speculations, my attempts to justify and make sense of events never stopped. Poles gave varying interpretations: "You were searched because you appeared nervous," and, "The search was definitely ordered in advance specifically for you. You are a suspicious person." There could not be any final interpretation.

Because of my experience leaving Poland in 1983, when I left in 1984, I was prepared. I was ready for 90 minutes of customs inspection, ready to be the last person to board the plane and to consume several drinks on the return flight. I would not allow the search to strip me of my dignity.

But nothing at all happened. The customs official did not open a single bag. Instead of inspecting my guitar, he asked with interest what kind it was. Did I play classical or folk music? He was polite and thanked me after the minute-long chat. I had a long wait in the restaurant before my plane took off, long enough to drink several beers and to purchase duty-free alcohol. Nothing had happened. No harassment. I had not had any problems. I felt great—even proud, like an ingenious Pole and honored guest of the Polish state!

The contrast between the two experiences illustrates the uncertainty ever-present in Polish life. There is no official word, only non-answers. The first experience at the airport was thoroughly humiliating. The latter experience was actually gratifying.

The Polish system sets people up to feel insecure and to keep them guessing. To expect the worst and to finagle for the best is all one can do. Humiliation is based on the fundamental uncertainty built into Polish life. It is the knowledge that anything can happen; there are no guaranteed ways of affecting the outcome. Humiliation is the means through which people are socialized into the system.

Humiliation begins in school, where, in order to get good grades, children are encouraged to learn a different perspective than the one they have learned at home, often from teachers who themselves may not believe what they teach. According to academics who sit on university admissions panels, the Polish educational system has been, to their dismay, "effective," because students have learned to follow a rote "public" line of thinking. Many complain that candidates for university studies in the social sciences and humanities increasingly answer questions without thinking, using instead accepted, official formulas.

In contrast to Western understanding of Eastern Europe, which emphasizes people's overt fear of the state and its apparatus, it is day-to-day humiliation that makes socialization effective. This humiliation is based on anger and frustration from constant wounded pride. As I learned from unpleasant first-hand experience, contact even with police begins, not necessarily with fear, but with humiliation.

Humiliation is one of the features of almost any contact with the formal organs of the state. In order to accomplish any bureaucratic or official matter, one must wait, often being ignored, rudely treated and incorrectly directed to a series of other offices. Poles are permanently dependent on people in offices who are doing their jobs as they please rather than according to their job description.

In such a system, people feel controlled by the whim and fancy of whoever happens to be in control in a given situation, be it the manager of a leather store, the customs officer at the airport or the clerk in a shoe store. If I manage to strike a private deal, I feel successful. There are few protective controls and guidelines, even for those who operate within the parameters of the system. People are protected only by private arrangements and by acquaintances.

Having finagled curtains for her apartment, Ala had mixed feelings about the way she had procured them. "I feel uneasy about it; it is against my dignity. I have a habit of doing bad things, and I am ashamed of myself," she conceded. But in the next breath, she justified her *na lewo* activity: "Ninety-nine percent of the curtains made in Poland go for export. If I didn't *załatwić* them through *znajomości* (contacts), I wouldn't be able to get curtains for five years. I realize that the situation put me to it." Ala feels a kind of revengeful pride—she is happy to manipulate a system that has humiliated her all her life.

The official ideology creates the impression that Ala can go into a state store to buy the curtains, and the clerk will sell them to her; a clerk sells goods to consumers. Yet both Ala and the clerk realize that it does not work that way. Private arrangements are vital to survival, yet people have some compunction about accomplishing day-to-day tasks *na lewo*. They take pride in having been *sprytny* (ingenious or clever in successfully arranging a deal), but this sort of achievement is, at the same time, an affront to their dignity and a source of guilt. While Poles feel powerful when they are *sprytny*, they also lose some self-respect. The way a *sprytny* individual is regarded reflects a conflicting moral code. There is admiration for him, but little respect. Being *sprytny* is not morally affirmed.

The ambivalent feelings which result from both pride and shame are demonstrated by the two distinctive meanings of the Polish term *normalny* (normal). According to the first meaning, "normal" is that which actually occurs most often and is therefore "typical." Hence, that Ala had to strike a deal with the clerk in order to get the curtains of her choice is normal. However, the second meaning, "as it ought to be," derives from a certain value of "how things should be," which reflects a common-sense understanding of how things should be. According to the second meaning, it is not at all normal that Ala had to strike a deal with the clerk in order to procure the curtains.

Officially, honesty is extolled as a main virtue, yet, in practice, the system encourages people to behave dishonestly. One hears such remarks: "I think I am as honest as others. I consider myself an honest person and that which I do is simply life." The backroom finagling necessary to acquire the trappings of a state-defined normal life produces an everyday existence that is anything but the officially defined normal. The humiliating need to make extensive, time-consuming private arrangements merely to acquire the goods and services that people feel ought to be easily obtainable is tension-producing and stressful.

Because Ala wanted a normal life (second meaning), including the ownership of decent curtains, she found it necessary to act in a normal way (first meaning), which made her feel ashamed. But because her accomplishment brought her closer to a normal (second meaning) life, she also felt proud. The ambivalent feelings of pride and shame, inextricably mixed, reflect how most Poles feel towards their everyday lives. Shame is born of the exhaustion and frustration produced by complete dependency on the whim and fancy of people in their official roles in the system, and on what one sometimes has to do. Pride is born of the pleasure of success in accomplishing a difficult task. Both dejection—impotence and frustration—and elation—a deviant sense of success—are typical of the way in which people in Poland react to managing everyday tasks.

BETWEEN MATERIAL AND SPIRITUAL

Despite psychological tension and practical difficulties in attaining a normal (second meaning) life, the material possessions associated with it are, for many people, just as important as personal and professional characteristics in determining the social standing of others. One mother asked a series of questions as she tried to assess whether the boyfriend of her engineer daughter would make a suitable husband: "Is he educated? Is he from a good family? Is he cultured? Does he drink? Does he have connections? Has he been abroad? Does he own a car? Does he have an apartment?" Favorably impressed that he had his own apartment, the mother wanted to know how many rooms the apartment had. The mother's questions were illustrative of the categories often used to gauge social position.

The most important material belongings are considered typically to be apartments and cars. Possessing any apartment is an accomplishment worthy of respect. A three-room dwelling is regarded as sizable. Car ownership is the second most important question concerning material and financial position.

Yet, in a world where homes, possessions and jobs can last for years or disappear overnight, personal and moral qualities remain a prime concern. Drinking is popular in Poland and central to many gatherings, but a "drunkard" is looked down upon. A person is considered "cultured" if he has refined language and manners, intellectual curiosity and knowledge of the arts.

Someone who is considered an intellectual by American standards often would be merely "cultured" by Polish ones. A "cultured" individual has almost always read much more world literature and history than an American scholar. He typically is more familiar with American literature than an American. He is knowledgeable about the latest world films, and has seen and discussed many of them. He frequently attends the theater, where he may meet his "cultured" acquaintances. Cultured status may involve speaking foreign languages, often French, English or German. Being cultured may mean having an established lineage, having attended the "right" secondary schools or having the "right" friends. It may also involve owning appropriate household furnishings, paintings and books.

Education carries more prestige in Poland than it does in the United States. "Educated" refers to anyone who had graduated from a university or technical institute of higher education. Yet education alone does not qualify a person as "cultured."

Part of a person's moral status is coming from a good family. In every social milieu or stable community in which families have known each other for many generations, certain families are considered good and certain ones bad. It was said about a prominent Polish journalist, "How can it be that he came from such a 'good family' and became an alcoholic?"

A good family may have a history of high moral standards, abilities and discipline for generations. As part of a cultural elite with a particular ethos, members of the traditional intelligentsia have a heritage of education, cultural competence and social service.

They are proud of their geneaologies and know them
well. One *inteligent* (member of the traditional intelligentsia) chronicled his family tree:

> My great-great grandfather was sent to Siberia about 100
> years ago for organizing socialist groups in Warsaw. That
> was the time of the beginning of the socialist movement,
> and he spent the next 30 years in Siberia. When the Rev-
> olution of 1905 started, he was a delegate to the council
> of workers in Moscow. In Moscow he became active in
> circles of Polish immigration. He organized material help
> and a Polish cultural center for political emigrees.
>
> His son, my great-grandfather, was also a very active
> person. He was a pediatrician. When the first Warsaw
> housing cooperative was started in the '20s, he organized
> a nursery and a school there. The housing cooperative was
> not only to provide people with apartments, but also to
> give them a whole community life.

The same *inteligent* spoke of his grandmother, a famous educator, and of his parents, both renowned
scholars active in public life.

A good family not only exhibits the right moral
characteristics, but is usually "well-situated" and often
has "connections."

The Roman Catholic Church has long guided Polish morality and spiritual values. Nearly 95 percent
of the populace is Catholic. With some 20 million
communicants each week, the Church is the institution that can claim the most widespread allegiance
in postwar Poland. During the Pope's historic visit
to Poland in June of 1983, police officials ordered
crowds congregating outside of his private quarters
to disperse. Their commands were ignored, and they
were forced to give up and turn the matter over to
Church officials. A priest stood before the crowd and
uttered one sentence, "We request that the crowd
please disperse." The crowd yielded without protest.

The Church is revered by the populace for its status as the only institution capable of challenging the

government. In 1984 the Church declared that the month of August was to be one of abstinence. As part of the Church's fight against alcoholism, people were not supposed to drink or purchase alcoholic beverages for the entire month. But during this month, state stores were stocked with fancy liquors, champagne and other specialty alcohols, which for years had not been available in such abundant supply. People said that the government thereby hoped to prove the Church a failure. One friend who liked to drink was upset by the "government's tactics" and resolved to "follow the Church." He arranged his vacation in West Germany, where drinking had no such politically charged anti-government overtones.

But while Poles appreciate the Church for its independent status, they are selective in their adherence to its teachings. People look to the Church for spiritual renewal, but its policies regarding alcoholism, divorce, sexual relations and abortion are only partially effective in urban areas. The Church speaks against divorce, yet official statistics show the rate is high; it preaches against the abuse of alcohol, yet Poles are among the world's leading consumers of vodka and alcoholism is rampant; the Church denounces premarital sex and abortion, yet, by the acknowledgement of Church documents and officials, both are common.

According to official statistics, over 300,000 abortions are performed in Poland each year. But official statistics include only those abortions performed in state hospitals. Many more go unreported, and unofficial sources speculate that the official number accounts for only one-third of those carried out. This is more than the annual number of live births. Numerous women speak of having had several abortions.

The Church has carried out aggressive anti-abortion and anti-birth control campaigns in recent years. Even so, the high rate of abortion is understandable.

In a country in which most other forms of birth control are often difficult to obtain or ineffective, abortion is a main means of birth control. In a country in which thousands of young people live in cramped quarters with no practical hope of obtaining their own apartment, many women have abortions out of economic necessity.

Economic realities are more effective social constraints than Church doctrines. One official of the Catholic Intelligentsia Club told me, "Many Poles are deeply religious, but this doesn't mean they follow Church policies. The influence of the Church against such things as divorce, abortion, birth control and sex outside of marriage is only partial and indirect."

The Church is a refuge for many. But, like the state, it is, for some, yet another source of shame. The tension between church teachings and the lifestyles encouraged under the conditions of People's Poland produces stress and guilt in many. As one friend put it, "Out of necessity many people do what the Church teaches against, but no one is proud of it."

*   *   *

A renewed emphasis on spiritual and intellectual qualities is the response of many to bureaucratic humiliation and national uncertainty. *Duchowe* is an adjective that means at once spiritual, intellectual, moral, mental, emotional, religious and "of the soul." English has no equivalent concept. In Poland emotional, spiritual and intellectual life are less compartmentalized. *Duchowe* life is the emotional and spiritual fiber of the private world. It allows one to escape from the psychological weariness produced by the realities of *złatwianie spraw*. Far removed from material concerns, *duchowe* life gives Polish culture its true flavor.

A crucial component of *duchowe* life, regardless of social status, is intellectual pursuit. Slavic countries have strong literary traditions—people *read*. That which is expressed verbally in political and social life in the West is put on paper in Slavic countries. That which is aired on television in the United States is published in articles in Poland.

Talented writers—of plays, films, novels, poems and nonfiction—are involved in social and political affairs and deal with these problems in their works. Theater almost invariably focuses on historical or current political and social themes. Poland's film idols are not glamorous screen stars but political-moral heroes. There is little tradition of "light theater" or "light film." As one writer put it, "Polish writers want to be saints—the voice of the nation."

Most Polish nationalist symbols come from literature. For instance, resistance conspirators of World War II chose their pseudonyms from names of patriotic heroes in historic novels of the Polish Nobel Prize-winning Henryk Sienkiewicz.

Poetry, in particular, expresses the longing for a national utopia and the struggle to achieve it. Traditionally, poetry has had an important function in the political and social spheres, which it never had in the Anglo-Saxon traditions.

In Poland every social group aspires to intellectual accomplishment. People read not merely as a pastime, but also to compare their life experiences with those people they are reading about and to participate in intellectual discussion. Hence, one can understand the disappointment of a secretary in my institute when I was unable to shed more light on the characters in *Gone with the Wind*, which she was reading for the third time, or the disappointment of my seamstress, a Hemingway fan, when I could not tell her much about Hemingway's life. One can also understand the utter disbelief of several friends that I had not read Karen Horney's books on neurosis in modern society; that I had read only two of Dostoyevski's works; that I could not remember the details of Joseph Conrad's *Lord Jim*, which Poles say depicts the moral complex of being Polish. One friend gave me a reading list so that I could better participate in *duchowe* life on my next trip to Poland.

A lawyer was surprised that professionals he had met in West Germany seemed narrowly educated and "knew little about the world." Given the rich Polish literary tradition, he was taken aback when West German lawyers asked him if Poland had produced any notable literature. He was astounded that educated professional people he had met in the United States were not able to discuss literature and did not know much about other countries. "An educated Pole, for example, could tell you where Sri Lanka is, the approximate population and basic geographical background," he told me. The lawyer's girlfriend added that, when she had lived in Canada, people asked her, "Where is Poland?" and, "Do they speak Russian there?"

Visiting scholars in Poland are pleasantly surprised to find a high level of interest in their scholarship. And many are envious of their Polish colleagues—for the public *cares* what they do and why. What one studies, reads, and writes matters. People respect ideas and are hungry for the written word.

Two friends—an engineer and a physician—spent hours one afternoon asking questions about Native American cultures, my experiences living among American Indians and the lifestyles of ancient Indian groups, as deduced from archeological sites in Mexico. They quizzed me about the "skinhead" and "new wave" movements of the United States and Western Europe. This thirst for information resulted partly from the fact that these two had not travelled to the West and had limited sources of information about life there. But the most important element in their desire to know was simply the value they placed on this kind of knowledge. It is *duchowe* life, not the latest VCR or new investment opportunities that makes their lives interesting.

Small private gatherings are an essential part of *duchowe* life. At such gatherings, people tell rich stories about their own and other's experiences. An elderly woman greeted me with kisses and compliments. After telling my fortune with cards, she talked for hours about such topics as the German occupation, a Russian escapee from a nearby concentration camp, her father, a Polish general who was killed in the first days of the war and the family's mansion, which they lost after the war. Her daughter and granddaughter chimed in periodically with questions: "How did they feed so many mouths on starvation ration cards? What games did they play and how did they pass the time?" The middle-aged journalist, whom I teased about his affairs with 20-year-old women, talked to me far into the night about his childhood years in a concentration camp.

Participation in intellectual life and discussion is a crucial component of social identity and reputation. A professor of sociology who was threatened with losing his job for political reasons was unconcerned about his future as a professional sociologist. He knew he would continue to read, to write and to meet with his friends for passionate discussion. Losing his job would not decrease his social standing, nor would he lose his authority as an intellectual. He would continue to participate in *duchowe* life.

Religious life is a vital part of *duchowe* life. The clergy stresses *duchowe* life, in this context meaning spirituality, to counterbalance the official media, which stress materialism. Since the imposition of martial law, Poles have become even more deeply involved in religion. In recent years numerous countries have seen dwindling recruitment into the Church, but Polish interest has expanded. The numbers of individuals entering the priesthood and the sisterhood increased throughout the 1970s and continues to do so.

In 1985, opposition leader Adam Michnik wrote about the place of the Church from prison for the *New York Review of Books:*

Church buildings ring with the free words of Polish literature and the sounds of Polish music, and their walls are
adorned with the works of Polish painters, not only because the Church has become an asylum for independent
Polish culture. The Church is the most important institution in Poland because it teaches all of us that we may
bow only before God.

Participation in religious activities and the invocation
of religious symbols has increased in the 1980s. The
turn to religion is discernible among all social groups.
A study published by a Catholic press attests to this
renewal:

> Recently there has been some religious animation among
> the intellectuals. Religiousness has also increased among
> workers. It may have been caused by the fact that a Pole
> was elected a Pope, that Pope John Paul II has visited his
> native country, that the Solidarity movement, standing
> close to the Church and supported by the Church, was
> born.

I observed a turn to religion during martial law,
even on the part of the intelligentsia. Some intellectuals, never before interested in the activities of the
Church and heretofore self-proclaimed atheists, have
experienced religious conversions.

The visit of the Pope to Poland in June of 1983
brought people to the streets in throngs. Unofficial
sources estimated that one-third of the population
actually saw the Pope during his weeklong tour.
Parishes and priests distributed some 100,000 entrance passes to the Pope's homily at Warsaw's stadium. But hundreds of thousands of people without
passes swarmed to the stadium to catch a glimpse of
the Holy Father.

I obtained one of the passes, and my experience
was an unforgettable ordeal. As thousands from all
over Poland attempted to crowd into the stadium,
the atmosphere was that of people trying to escape
in an emergency from a packed train or bus. It was

impossible to move in any direction. Thousands of people pressed against each other, frantically trying to move through the crowd. Groups of individuals forced their way through. As I stood in the crowd, it seemed ribs were crushed, arms broken, egos insulted. Hysteria reigned. Officials standing above crowds on ladders pleaded with the crowds to not push, to move slowly. Officials were to limit the number of people allowed into the stadium and justified this with "we have orders from above only to let a certain number of people through at one time," but elderly women pleaded, "Well, it only depends on you, *only* on you. Just let *us* through. Can't just *we* go through? Can you please . . ."

The crowd seemed eternally oppressive. But the moment the Pope uttered his first word, the screaming, shouting and shoving gave way to an awesome silence. One hundred thousand people in the stadium and some million people surrounding it listened in total quiet. The noise of trams from several miles away could be heard.

As I began to leave the stadium, before the mass had come to an end, the Pope started to pray. Thousands on the outskirts of the stadium spontaneously knelt in prayer. At one point Janusz and I realized we were the only ones moving—hundreds of thousands of people were kneeling in the streets. We, too, stopped and knelt until the prayer was completed.

For many Poles the Church is a refuge; it provides personal solace in times of economic and political upheaval. As one friend put it, "The Church is the only place where I feel safe."

The difficulties and uncertainties of life—the lack of correlation between efforts and results—encourages a faith in fate and destiny, and a "live for the moment" approach to life. People often explain what has happened in their lives in terms of "human destiny." The lack of control people feel they have over their lives is related to romantic notions about fortune, destiny, happiness and love, which are abundant in Polish culture. People say about themselves and others that they were "destined to be unhappy," "destined to leave Poland," or "destined to have misfortune." At an emotional private gathering lasting late into the night, a woman spoke of destiny. It was her own sad destiny to have been recently widowed. Her daughter, married and divorced three times, was "destined not to find love."

Some people attend and hold frequent parties, consuming rationed meat and spending scarce money on expensive liquor. They explain their actions with, "I earn so little money that there is no point in saving it," or, "Tomorrow there will be a war, and I will lose everything anyway." One 25-year-old compared national characters. "Germans live in order to save their money, to eat and to sweep the sidewalks," he said. "Poles live to have a good time and to spend all of their money on parties." He talked of how his grandparents bought back his mother from the Germans. She had been picked up in a systematic roundup of people in the streets of Warsaw. Her family had been very wealthy but had lost everything in the war. Such had been the family's destiny. "It doesn't depend on the individual, how his life will be, only on a greater power," he concluded.

Poles do not trust that life deals out justice. People do not believe that they deserve what they get or get what they deserve. In recent years, this disposition has become more pronounced. One result is an increase in fortune-telling and astrology. There is a growing fatalism about domestic and international threats, such as nuclear war. As Pani Janina explained, "We have no control over these things. Whatever happens happens; this is not our problem—no solution, no problem."

People are perpetually prepared for a quick turn of events that may change their lives overnight. A physicist who came to the United States as a visiting scholar stayed with an upper middle-class family for several weeks. She was puzzled that the 16-year-old daughter could be so certain of her future, believing she will marry a rich man, have a car and a home. "How can she be so sure?" my friend wanted to know, explaining that since she was a toddler she had learned that anything can happen and that what she knows, not what she has, is important. "I have an apartment in Poland, and I enjoy it, but I know I could lose it," she declared. "I could also lose my job."

PRIDE AND SHAME

The frequent conflict between material needs and spiritual values in everyday life is not the only contradiction in the Polish world. While many Poles feel inferior to the people of the West, Poles are at the same time proud patriots. They are simultaneously proud and ashamed of themselves and their nation.

Polish psychologist Zbigniew Nęcki studied how Poles assess their homeland and to what extent their way of thinking is influenced by impressions of the countries with which they compare their own. In a 1984 article printed in the official press, Nęcki wrote, "We compare ourselves to Western countries, the most developed ones such as the United States, Japan, France, Sweden, and the Federal Republic of Germany." Nęcki characterized the predominant popular stereotype he encountered among Poles as "poor but proud."

Many Poles admire and envy the West, not only for its ideology of freedom and democracy, but also for the abundance and prosperity it represents. Polish-style prosperity is a peculiar blend of Western stereotypes and Polish ingenuity. Many Poles feel about the West as many Americans feel about "romantic" Europe; they value Western goods as Americans value French perfume. Associations with the West—from Western products and fads to friends or relatives residing in the West—are status symbols and sources of pride.

Polish popular magazines and newspapers nurture Poles' infatuation with the West and its popular culture and personalities. According to officials of the Central Statistical Office, three women's magazines—*Kobieta i Życie (Woman and Life), Przyjaciółka (Woman Friend),* and *Gospodyni (Housewife)*—enjoy among the widest circulation of any publications in Poland, and are very widely read. In content, they resemble popular American magazines—a cross between *Ladies Home Journal* and *Cosmopolitan.* In *Kobieta i Życie,* I learned just what vitamins to take for "nerves" and what eye makeup to use for the particular shape of my eyes. I was informed of the latest Parisian fashions, adopted by the Polish jet set and how to sew them at home, since they are difficult to come by in state stores. I was advised on how to prepare cucumbers in mustard sauce, told that women began wearing brassieres only 80 years ago, and was provided with an update of the lives of Ernest Hemingway's granddaughters. I was informed of the latest films, affairs, children and sentiments of Sophia Loren, Debra Winger, Tony Curtis, Barbara Streisand, Joan Collins and Kate Jenkins. Yet I did not learn comparable gossip about actors and actresses from Poland or other East European countries. Perhaps ironically, Poles' taste for the West is often whetted by the Polish press.

Western products are the most noticeable status symbols in Poland. A store near my apartment had mostly empty shelves but featured a display window of empty cans of West German beer, crushed Coke and Seven-Up cans, and empty Marlboro and Dun-

hill cigarette cartons. The managers were proud of
the display. Similarly, "Kansas" cigarettes were introduced in Poland only recently and have become
quite popular. They are manufactured in the Neth-
erlands and sold in Pewex stores for dollars. Advertising posters feature a cowboy sitting on his horse
on the Great Plains smoking a cigarette, with the
slogan "Kansas Cigarettes—Real American Cigarettes."

Western standards and symbolic associations are
also evident in fashion ideals. For many Polish women,
the most flattering compliment would be, "In your
elegant dress you would fit in perfectly on the streets
of Paris." The customers of my seamstress choose
from fashions featured in Spiegel's, Sears' and Pen-
ney's catalogues, as well as in *Vogue, Cosmopolitan,
People* and *Ladies Home Journal* magazines. Customers
determine the latest fashion by viewing pictures of
celebrities and models in advertisements.

Many Polish citizens earn status in the eyes of their
peers by having studied, worked, or travelled in the
West and by having Western friends. Several times,
I was being entertained by friends in their homes
when other guests came to call. They were told, "I
can't invite you in today. I have guests from abroad."
Having an association of some kind with the West—
relatives, travel experiences, knowledge of English
or French, possession of Western products—is, for
many Poles, a source of pride.

While emulating the West is important for almost
everyone's cultural status, Poles who aspire to be part
of the ruling elite must guide their careers under Soviet constraints. Ironically, those whose success has
been in the army, police, Communist Party or government are often the first to boast of a dress from
Paris or to recount tales of a recent trip to London.
In a provincial town, I saw rural dwellers and
townspeople waiting in corridors to take care of bureaucratic matters at their area's administrative cen-

ter. They were clad in the traditional black suits, white polyester shirts and hats, while the bureaucrats and Party officials with equivalent incomes wore Western jeans and imported clothes purchased in Pewex for dollars. The young women waiting in line wore whatever was available and no make-up. Women bureaucrats used many cosmetics and wore a "casual" jeans look. A Western pop music record filled the air.

Being known in the West confers status on a Pole. A woman who works in the Party apparatus was eager for her son to appear on an American television program: "His career could be made *in Poland* by appearing on such a show," she said.

For many Poles the West is a paradise. For some, particularly people who have never travelled to the West, it provides an image of "the good life," of a place where life is easy or where there is less hardship. But the stereotype of the West is changing. One currently hears: "In the West one has to work very hard, but at least one has something to show for his labor."

As I visited a working class family one weekend in Lublin, the conversation centered around whether it is better to leave the country or stay in Poland. Family members, none of whom had been abroad, took turns telling stories of friends and acquaintances who had left the country. Over vodka, one sister said, "It's certainly better to leave Poland." She recited the list of friends who had sent word to their families in Poland that everything was fine. "They left only four months ago, and after working only that long, they *already* have an apartment and a car. They even send relief packages back to their families." Another sister said, "I don't think I could leave permanently. I think I would miss my family and my country." But she shared the success stories of her own friends and agreed that it was "really best to leave Poland."

Many Poles cast an uncritical eye on the West, imagining it to be an improved Poland. Some emigrate in search of a better Poland but instead find a complex, lonely world, devoid of the *duchowe* life they were accustomed to at home. Still, they remain abroad. The words of a mother exemplify the prevailing attitude in Poland. After her young son moved permanently to the United States, she commented, "The best way to succeed in Poland is to leave it for the West."

Indeed, in contact with other nationalities, Poles often express shame about being Polish. Forty-four percent of Nęcki's respondents indicated they were ashamed of being Poles in some circumstances. The source of this shame was, according to Necki, "everyday situations that they had encountered abroad or about which they had heard." Some were ashamed that they had behaved in an "undignified" manner to acquire material benefits. In the company of foreigners and while travelling abroad, Poles sometimes feel their "Polishness" to be an inferior quality.

Yet, Poles almost invariably express national pride. There is an underlying pride in the sentiment: "Only we know how things really are; everyone else is naive. We know how to *załatwić*; we know how to live."

An American stopped in Warsaw on his way back from a two-week trip to the Soviet Union, which he described as "filled with moving experiences." One evening he eagerly shared his "revelations" about the Soviet Union with Polish guests at a party. This irritated other Americans in the group, who had lived in Poland for several years and realized that Poles, with the Soviet Union as neighbor, are acutely aware of East-bloc realities. "The Soviet Union is not black and it's not white," said the American swayed by his own sentiment. "It's red," resounded one of the Poles. We all roared. Though I was embarrassed by the American storyteller for his naivete, the Poles were not; they responded to the American's stories as to those of a child. They did not expect more sophistication from the visitor. The Poles took pride in knowing what the situation was—in their superior knowledge and understanding.

Nęcki says that Poles reaffirm their sense of national pride "with the selection of a Polish Pope, the events of August, 1980 and various sports events." Poles I met felt a similar pride in the awarding of the Nobel Peace Prize to Lech Wałęsa. The Solidarity period and its aftermath, with Western journalists flocking to Poland by the dozens, inspired national pride. Some Solidarity activists proudly display books about Solidarity and the "Polish crisis" published in the West. Such recognition serves as one sanction of their sentiments.

These recent events have revitalized national pride, but the foundation of this pride stretches back for centuries. Nęcki notes that in his survey, ". . . the combative spirit of the Polish soldier was often quoted as a reason for national pride." The Polish sense of history is at the root of the pride Poles feel in their nation and themselves.

UNDER THE POWER OF THE PAST

The past has taught Poles how to adjust and live with a difficult situation. It has given them a model for coping with hardship and grief. The past is an inescapable nightmare. But it is also a source of sustenance and serves as an explanation for a current situation which many people find difficult. Though Poles remain ambivalent about having to operate in such an environment, they are masters of contradiction and successful actors within its bounds.

The declaration of martial law on December 13, 1981 shocked the populace and formed a landmark in the lives of citizens, yet Poles celebrated Christmas two weeks later in almost normal fashion. The deep tremor had brought everything to a halt and forced many people to abandon their agendas and reorient their lives. About 5,000 people were interned. Some people lost jobs or worried that they would lose them; military discipline was introduced at work. Emigration and trips abroad were cancelled automatically. Life plans and expectations were dampered. An atmosphere of hope and excitement was replaced by one of hardship and despair. People learned of the fundamental revision in their lives when they heard the knock on the door in the night, turned on the radio or looked out on the street to see tanks on the morning of December 13th.

How is it, then, that Poles tried to celebrate Christmas, the most important Polish holiday, almost two weeks later in the usual fashion, in spite of a curfew (except on Christmas Eve to accomodate the traditional midnight mass), identification checks, travel restriction, imposing police and military presence and profound uncertainty? Poles scurried around, trying to procure as many as available of the 12 traditional Christmas Eve dishes: herring in oil, potato and apple salad, dried mushroom soup, red borsht, three kinds of carp in jelly or fried carp, cabbage with mushrooms, perogi with mushrooms, dumplings with poppy seed, compote with dried apples, pears, and plums, and cake, tea and fruit. As usual, they invited family over for celebration on Christmas Eve and on the first day of Christmas and friends for the second day of Christmas festivities.

The task of adjusting to the demands of life-jolting turns of events and potentially life-threatening circumstances has become an art, honed over years of experience. People have become accustomed to dramatic and tragic situations. That Poles celebrated Christmas in somewhat normal fashion indicated not an acceptance of martial law, but rather a seasoned ability to adapt. "When you are among crows, you have to crow like they do," says a Polish proverb. The hard facts of Polish life have engendered a culture of survival. The longevity of the Polish memory provides a firm foundation for Poles' current responses which enable them to persevere through times of crisis and uncertainty. A history of hardship has cultivated ingenuity.

Knowledge of a difficult past, preserved for generations by means of patriotism and piety, not only feeds resilient idealism—so much a part of the Polish national character—but also facilitates material survival. Poles appreciate the art of adjustment but are forever critical of it as detrimental to the spirit.

"Without Christ, one can't understand events in Poland," reads a plaque underneath a crucifix in a church of Warsaw's Old Town. Vanguarded by the Church and spurred on by nationalist fervor, Poles to this day remain stubborn loyalists to the idea of a Polish nation and to the Church itself, which has provided an organizational forum for resistance and a wellspring of nationalism.

The contradictions between the public face of Poland and the private lives of its citizens are hardly new. Poles had already developed a national consciousness when Poland was partitioned among Russia, Prussia and Austria in 1792 (the Prussian territories were conquered by Germany in 1870); but Poland did not reemerge as a recognized state until 1918. Poland, with her experience as a nation under external rule, has long had two faces.

The country has a long history of informal, extralegal networking. From 1792 to 1918, when Poland was partitioned, legal systems associated with the state were regarded as symbols of the occupying country's power; lack of respect for these legal institutions was seen as a patriotic act.

A Polish peasant who lived in the German partition, Michał Drzymała, has become a popular folk hero because of his legal dispute with German authorities. Since a law passed in 1904 prohibited Polish peasants from building homes or barns on land purchased from Germans, Drzymała decided to live in a covered cart on his property. When the authorities charged that the cart, stationed in one location was an "illegal building," Drzymała moved the cart each day to a different place on the property. Having no legal grounds to remove the cart, it was only after five years that the Germans overstepped their own laws and removed it by force. Though, in the end, the Germans won, according to public opinion, the *sprytny* (clever) Polish peasant was victorious. He had flouted the legalistic German system successfully.

It was during the partitions that an entire informal system of extralegal relationships was elaborated. On several occasions, most notably in 1794, 1830 and 1863, Poles led insurrections against foreign oppressors which were aimed toward overthrowing the existing social order. Defiance of the official legal system and social order provided the genesis for these national uprisings.

From 1918 to 1939, attempts were made to construct an effective state bureaucracy and a viable industrial base. Poles had relative success in establishing an independent, legitimate state, but it did not prove to be strong enough to maintain independence. Under German occupation from 1939 to 1945, Poles were again faced with a foreign government and had to rely on Polish ways of surviving. The German occupation suspended further the social and legal norms of the previous era.

For Poles the German occupation was a time when millions met their death through slave labor and starvation. Underground networks resisted both the occupying Germans and the advancing Russians. The extensiveness of the informal economy is well-documented in diaries and memoirs written by Poles who lived in German-occupied Poland. Many present-day terms for getting by—*załatwić, kombinować, zorganizować*—can be found in these records. Those who survived the concentration camps, slave labor and scarcities of World War II did so through bribery and black market activities. An article published in August of 1945, shortly after the end of the war, described common survival strategies. In the literary journal *Twórczość*, the prominent literary critic Kazimierz Wyka wrote:

> The population had to choose between eating what they were allowed to, and starving to death [ration allocations were too small for actual needs], or managing somehow. Nobody considered the first alternative seriously—the only important question was *how* to manage in spite of the regulations.

Wyka characterized the many laws and policies implemented by the Nazi *Generalgouvernement*, including the rationing system and the prohibition of selling and buying agricultural products, as "social fiction." The years of the occupation actually saw, as Wyka described it, an elaborate "excluded economy."

People held unofficial jobs and used their official jobs as a base for black market activity. According to historian Jan Tomasz Gross, legitimate businesses dealt on the black market, maintaining two bookkeeping systems and two wage scales. Unofficial benefits for workers in some jobs included free dinners or working hours and space in which to conduct private business. In many workplaces, employers and managers tolerated absenteeism. Gross concludes:

> It was perfectly normal for a worker to show up at his place of work for only about four days a week, so that the rest of his time could be devoted to the black market. A joke popular at the time describes the situation fairly. Two

friends who had not seen each other for a long time met
on the street:
    "What are you doing?"
    "I am working in the city hall."
    "And your wife, how is she?"
    "She is working in a paper store."
    "And your daughter?"
    "She is working in a plant."
    "How the hell do you live?"
    "Thank God, my son is unemployed."

Even in the most totalitarian of systems, wrote
Wyka in 1945, "the occupying force could not control everything." Wyka described a "psychological
residue" from the war that has an important role in
the post-war period.

Poland's "excluded economy" persists long after
the extreme conditions which encouraged its existence have disappeared. The trade which enabled
many to survive the occupation—during which one-
fifth of the population perished—continues. Wyka
comments:

> Polish society [now holds] the conviction that the most
> important function in modern economy is trade, but of
> the most individual type.

After the war, Soviet-style political and economic
institutions—state planning, centralization, and the
one party system—were imposed on a country with
vastly different cultural institutions. This encouraged continued development of extralegal networking and of a system in which individuals deal with
official constraints and public chaos through private
means.

Past experience affords Poles the ability to make
down-to-earth adjustments to ensure a measure of
prosperity and survival. Knowledge of a proud past
feeds the resilient idealism that is part of the Polish
national character. Defiance has been cultivated
through centuries of foreign domination. The Polish

ethos, "We have always been dominated," which one hears repeatedly, expresses a recurrent national sentiment: that the Polish nation has failed to achieve prosperity and democratic ideals.

Poems of contemporary writers such as Czesław Miłosz, as those of the greatest Polish poet, Adam Mickiewicz (1798–1855), serve as a kind of national rhetoric. The works of Mickiewicz expressed the psychological predicament of Polish conspirators during the partitions, a predicament which has become a permanent element in Polish history.

With an honorable end in mind—freedom—Polish adolescents participated in underground or resistance activities and were considered heroes. An American might consider such a conspiracy "immoral" because of the means necessary to achieve the end. Conspiracy requires duplicity. It requires that real activities and values be secret, and that public appearances be false masks. Moreover, in periods of terror—as during the Second World War—conspirators were forced to grapple with the morality of death: The adolescent terrorist who killed, endangered himself and others in the process.

There was no way for Poles to fight for independence without such an "immoral" conspiracy. In his famous poem "To A Polish Mother" (1830), Mickiewicz contrasted a Polish patriot with soldiers of the American Revolution:

> He [a Polish patriot] will be challenged by an unknown spy [for the partitioning powers], perjurious justice will fight with him, a secret grave will serve as the battlefield, and the powerful enemy [authorities of the partitions] will sentence him.
> He will learn to conceal his anger under the ground, be as enigmatic as the devil, to poison [others] with his words like foul vapor, and to appear as modest as a cold snake.

Mickiewicz compared the martyrdom of the Polish nation to the crucifixion of Christ—but without hope of resurrection:

Though the whole world will bloom in peace, though all governments and peoples and outlooks will concur, your son [of a "Polish mother"] will be challenged to fight without glory, and to martyrdom without resurrection.

One morning, a very loud alarm sounded in the city of Toruń, where I was visiting friends. A 59-year-old woman jumped up from the sofa where she had been sleeping and quickly downed a shot of cognac to soften the blow. A war had begun, she thought. The mentality of coping was so ingrained into her way of thinking that her first reaction was to reach for something which would lessen the blow and thereby enable her to respond lucidly. It was only a few seconds later that she realized the noise was a nearby burglar alarm.

On August 1, the anniversary of the beginning of the Warsaw uprising of 1944, the city's residents commemorate the dead by visiting the army cemetery. Though people flock to the cemetery en masse, silence prevails. Candles and flowers adorn the area, providing night lighting for the thousands of anonymous graves—small crosses made of simple stone lined up row after row and marked "unknown soldier." People wait in line to bless the graves. Elderly women, wiping their eyes, sit on benches at the foot of the graves of their lost sons and husbands.

"History, memory is our wealth," says one Polish woman. Memorials to historic events are found throughout Poland, and many visit the sites.

Poles reminisce about the past and celebrate memories of it. Almost every 100 yards on busy streets in central Warsaw, the site of the uprising, one sees stone markers attached to the walls of buildings. The memorials are draped with the Polish flag, adorned with flowers and lighted with candles. The markers commemorate the martyrdom of those who fell in the war, were shot by Germans during the occupation or died during the Warsaw uprising.

Each year, a memorial to the Warsaw uprising is

built in an old warehouse in Warsaw. The annual memorial is for Poles, not foreigners. The explanations are written in Polish; foreigners would find it difficult to follow the exhibit.

The display opens on August 1 and closes on October 2, the day the underground Home Army surrendered after almost one quarter of a million Poles, most of them civilians, had been killed.

The exhibit draws large crowds daily. Young and old visit the museum. Groups of Polish girl scouts clad in grey uniforms and matching knee socks view photographs and listen to recorded protest songs. Visitors walk between barbed wire fences and street barricades built of pavement stones and sandbags, a recreation of the streets of Warsaw under siege. Inside the warehouses are photographs of those who fought and died in the uprising. Each room contains pictures of a separate section of Warsaw, divisions which remain to this day. The sections were preserved during the rebuilding of Warsaw, most of which lay in ruins at the end of World War II.

The atmosphere is reverent and somber. Old women and men, some with damp eyes, others weeping outright, stand motionless before photographs of a day they remember. Children look at the photographs of the ruins in which their particular section of the city lay 40 years ago. They see young children and teenagers carrying guns and wearing cumbersome helmets above dirty faces. They see young women scurrying with fresh water and underground messages and old men setting up barricades. An occasional picture of a woman or man smiling reminds one that these people *lived* amid this chaos—they ate, quarreled, and made love among devastation and ruin. Beneath the pictures lie bouquets of flowers, often already wilted.

From cradle to grave, Poles are inundated with stories of their own history. Allegiance to the Church is in large part a product of Poles' sense of history. Solidarity astutely held its demonstrations on the anniversaries of past national uprisings. Churches exhibited displays commemorating historically relevant dates, expounding on the power of the past in present-day Poland.

A boy whose sister had just been arrested by martial law authorities exclaimed, "This is just like the time of the partitions, when people had no rights." After reporting the event to the Church network concerned with political detainees, he said, "Oh, it's not so bad. Maybe she'll be gone for only a few months."

This boy was just 11 years old, but he knew well the story of his great-grandfather, who had been deported to Siberia, and his grandfather, who had perished in Auschwitz. His young memory stretched back several hundred years. The partitioning powers of the eighteenth and nineteenth centuries, exile in Siberia, death in Auschwitz and martial law internment were not remote horrors from history books or movies but part of the reality of his life. Knowing there could be no appeal, he concluded simply, "My sister has bad luck."

6

Entangled Affiliations

As I walked through the deserted narrow streets of Warsaw one evening in 1982, only a half year after the imposition of martial law, I heard elated shouts and moans of disappointment coming from hundreds of individual apartments. Family and friends, glued to black-and-white television sets, crowded the rooms of small apartments. For lack of sitting space, some sat on window sills, backs to the street outside. The enthusiastic outbursts were responses to the Polish soccer team's plays during the World Cup soccer championship, held every four years.

The sports event provided a welcome diversion from a tense atmosphere and constant political talk. Everyone watched—it was impossible to find a cab that evening. Almost all Poles—young and old, underground and government supporters—were vocally united behind the national soccer team.

With the exception of popular and jazz music concerts, such as the annual Jazz Jamboree festival in Warsaw, and some religious ceremonies such as the annual pilgrimage to Częstochowa, the only times emotions—usually reserved for private life—are undeniably expressed in the public domain is when people are watching sports events. Spectator sports are the only activities in which almost the entire society can safely join together in passionate public demonstration. Sports are apolitical, yet nationalis-

tic. Everyone can rally behind them with wild enthusiasm, free of the caution and restraint that per-
vade almost every other arena of Polish life, where
people are always aware of internal politics.

I asked a close friend if she would allow me to do
an untaped interview with her. When she seemed
reluctant, I assured her, "It's not about politics."

"But it's hard to separate my life from politics,"
she replied. "The way I live is connected with politics. The kind of apartment I have, the fact that I'm
not married, the circumstances of my life cannot be
separated from politics. Even if something about my
private life seems absolutely unrelated to politics,
others might interpret it in political terms. That's why
I'd like to avoid the interview."

I did not go to Poland as a "crisis analyst," or to
study politics per se. Yet political activity and uncertainty permeated the atmosphere. Had I tried to avoid
politics in my study of cultural, social and economic
Poland, my understanding would have indeed been
limited. Politics and social life are inextricably bound.
In recent years, political views and affiliations have
impinged on arenas that formerly were defined primarily by their social or cultural characteristics.

HELP EACH OTHER

In September of 1980 a challenge to the state system appeared. From the midst of turbulent economic
and political conditions, there arose a grass roots organization which would provide a major, but short-
lived, challenge to the structure of Polish society.

During my stay in martial law Poland, I was often
told, "Too bad you weren't in Poland during the
Solidarity period. You missed the exciting times."

Solidarity emerged as a legal organization with the

signing of the Gdańsk accords between representatives of the Inter-factory Strike Committee and those of the Polish government. Unprecedented in East European postwar history, the signing of the accords followed a series of crippling nationwide labor strikes—which had begun in July of 1980—and several weeks of intense negotiations. Solidarity set up headquarters in Gdańsk and regional organizations throughout the entire country, and by the time it was declared an illegal organization with the imposition of martial law one and one-half years later, approximately 10 million people (about two-thirds of the working population) had become members.

Solidarity stood for "renewal" in social, political and economic life. It promoted an ideology of openness and accountability. In its ideology, it stood against the ways of *załatwić* and protested the means necessary to achieve a "normal" life. The movement thereby brought conflicts intrinsic to the everyday lives of most Poles into public consciousness and open discussion.

Solidarity fought against the constant ambivalence and humiliation people experience when dealing with the state bureaucracy and economic constraints. Stefan Bratkowski, a prominent journalist who was expelled from the Party after the declaration of martial law, called Solidarity "a revolution of common sense." Humiliation is an important but subtle means of state socialization in Poland; Solidarity's insistence on dignity was therefore threatening. Soliditary's platform read:

> Our birth was a protest against wrongs, humiliation and injustice. We are an independent, self-governing labor union of working people from all regions and all vocations. We defend the rights, dignity and interests of the entire working world. . . .
> We base social justice on the principle of the natural *dignity of the human being, of the working man and of his labor*. It is our wish that the principle of man's dignity permeate

everything about our union and serve as the foundation upon which relations in the new society are built.

Solidarity uplifted the dignity so central to Polish morality and used the phrase "to regain dignity" widely as its statement of purpose. To support dignity was to encourage the power of society and to challenge that of the state.

The "corruption" and special privileges enjoyed in the 1970s by the government of Edward Gierek came to be a popular target. Both the official media and the Solidarity press directed allegations against many top government and Party officials.

Solidarity's platform articulated people's deep-seated resentment towards the ruling elite.

> People in the power apparatus make decisions from the standpoint of their personal interests, material privileges and advancement rather than with respect to society's interests. The erroneous decisions on investments . . . and foreign loans that frequently go to waste have repeatedly resulted from the maneuvering of interest groups, supporting or fighting each other, within the power apparatus. From 1976–1979, economic bureaucrats frustrated, for the most part, any measures that might have prevented the crisis. As a rule, the bureaucratic apparatus opposed any change or reform that might undermine its own position, income or influence.

Solidarity shook the foundations of ruling elite "corruption," denouncing high-ranking government officials, some of whom were subsequently stripped of their titles and ousted from the Party.

In its rhetoric, the Church affirmed Solidarity's challenge. During Pope John Paul II's 1983 visit to martial law Poland, the church newspaper *Tygodnik Powszechny* said his message focused on:

> . . . man, on human dignity, on human beings' inalienable rights, on man's duty to show solidarity and resist any wrong, oppression or injustice. . . . on the dig-

nity of human labor and the accompanying rights of working people.

Inspired by the Pope's dictum, workers insisted on dignity: "Work shouldn't destroy a person. Work is for people, not people for work." Dignity—the antithesis of humiliation—came to be a central rallying call of Solidarity's challenge.

Solidarity propagated the ideal, "help each other," and propelled into the public consciousness the idea of public solutions to common individual problems. The open atmosphere of the Solidarity period created the conditions for an explosion of neighborhood and local self-government activities.

To an outside observer, Solidarity's existence was paradoxical. The organization rose to power at a time of increasing shortages, and, though it supported the idea of public solutions, its members could not have persisted without the family-based strategies of *załatwić*. Solidarity developed precisely because of the existence of the exchange networks and private problem-solving strategies that it opposed. Informal connections, in fact, served as a main organizing means within the movement. Solidarity's ideology stood against the fragmentation of society. Its platform read:

> The idea of uniting working people grants great importance to the value of common efforts. This value is represented by *Solidarność*—a term that we have adopted as the name of our labor union—and by good fellowship, the ability to make sacrifices and to do everything for the labor union community and for broader social interests. The idea of the working people's brotherhood as a common front against exploitation, no matter what mottos are used to disguise such exploitation, is part of this value.

Solidarity encouraged relationships extending beyond a small group of family and close friends. Though primarily a workers' movement, it also broke down social barriers between members of different social classes. Four years earlier, prominent intellectuals had created some links between isolated bastions of dissent among the intelligentsia, workers and farmers. For the first time, Solidarity brought together people from these groups en masse. The very idea of such connections was new, especially in a state accustomed to social isolation and traditional class barriers.

The formal prohibition of Solidarity has encouraged a retreat to private Poland—to acknowledged reliance on family-based survival strategies for dealing with pervasive problems. It has forced a return to separate private and public worlds, and to social and class isolation. Solidarity's ideology of "help each other," an ideology of an open society, did not belong in the world of martial law. But those tied to underground networks could still be expected to "help each other" across social and class barriers, carrying out clandestine activities.

THE POWER OF HONOR

With an ominous display of force, General Jaruzelski and his colleagues imposed martial law in December of 1981 to consolidate their power. The West has heard much about the immediate results of this measure—demonstrations, tear gas, street battles, arrests, internment. The national underground leadership was unable to command effective nationwide resistance. But the populace drew on the tradition of symbolic opposition, often without practical effect. For "honor," an important value guiding Polish life, people have sacrificed their personal freedom, economic interests and even their lives.

In the early weeks of martial law, a Solidarity activist purposely arrived at the doorstep of the apartment of a Solidarity leader who it was reasonable to assume had been arrested. The activist went, knowing full well that policemen were likely waiting for whoever might come to the apartment. He went as a matter of honor. He was taken into custody immediately. "I was rather conscious I might pay the price," he told me.

The activist had been separated from his wife for a number of months and divorce proceedings were underway. But when the wife learned of her husband's arrest, she immediately halted them. Her action, she explained, was also "a matter of honor."

A man with a British girlfriend was interned during martial law. The girlfriend suspected that his family's apartment was under police surveillance, and, being fearful, she did not visit the family. She did, however, send letters and gifts to them through mutual friends. But when the man was released several months later, he was angry and reluctant even to speak to her.

Visiting his family while he was imprisoned was "a matter of honor," he insisted. He was indignant because she had not been "loyal" to his family. The British woman was dumbfounded, since she had reasoned that the boyfriend would be pleased she had not risked her right to stay in Poland so they could be together upon his release. But the relationship was over.

The boyfriend told her harshly: "My best friend Jacek could have avoided my family's apartment because he was afraid of being associated with me. He could have said, 'My wife is pregnant. I can't afford to go to an apartment under surveillance now because it might create problems not only for me, but also for my wife and child.' But instead he came to the apartment every day to see if there was anything he could help my mother with. You must understand that in this situation all actions are of great significance—how you behave, how you conduct yourself, who you visit, who you don't visit—these are all very important actions."

One activist explained the importance of "solidarity" among the opposition.

> It's necessary to help others and to be with others. If someone fails to help, this destroys the community, not mainly because it leaves people without resources—coffee, chocolate and cigarettes are of little importance. The minimum one must do is to be with people, which involves *not* saying 'I'm afraid—I can't talk with you now because you're suspected.' If I neglect someone who is close to me just because he is in political trouble, then the system is victorious. What would happen if everyone were afraid of helping each other—what would happen to Polish society?

Lending moral and material support to internees and their families was of great importance. One internee wrote in a letter smuggled out of prison during martial law:

> My family receives a lot of help—mostly food parcels from abroad and from many other people. Farmers supply internees' families with food, people bring money, thousands want to help. My mother once refused to accept another chicken from peasants—the refrigerator was full up. And we here enjoy the results of such help. We have coffee, chocolate, tea, foreign cheese, honey—in a country where such things are more easily found in museums than stores. "Oh shit, another Earl Grey Tea," exclaimed my friend two days ago. We are the focus of the most beautiful qualities of the nation. Helping us and our families is the most noble and patriotic task now. What a wonderful feeling to know about it, to experience it, to know that people care and remember.

Relatively few people participated in demonstrations and strikes, but many championed acts of defiance, at the same time acknowledging that they were politically futile. Indeed, the style of protest action was often more important than the results of the actions. Even school children became involved in protests. They protested the 9:00 P.M. curfew for children (in effect during part of martial law) by blinking lights on and off in their apartments and blowing whistles each evening at the curfew hour. From my apartment building I heard the sound of whistles and saw flickering light from tall block apartment buildings all around me.

Much of the long-standing conflict between the two polarized camps—the ruling elite and the opposition—is a symbolic one of competing ideologies, rhetoric and language, through which each side attempts to shape citizens' values and guide public behavior. Though they can never be part of the government, opposition leaders have a permanent role in public life in attempting to influence public opinion.

Each camp produces its own opinion-makers who aspire to be accepted by the people as *the* competent experts with blueprints for social and economic progress. Each side promotes its own national symbols, heroes and interpretations of history and Polish character. The ruling elite has used "national character" as a weapon on the ideological battleground. Articulating his own feelings, one friend voiced the ruling elite's view of Polish national character.

> A Pole is a typical romantic. A Pole never manages to think politically. Poles were always insurgents; a bottle of gas in one hand was their strength. Solidarity didn't manage to think politically either. In Poland if someone yells the word "freedom," everyone goes with him, but no one asks where he is going, what he hopes to accomplish or how long it will take.

The ruling elite's interpretation of history perpetuates the myth that Poles are anarchists, that they are not capable of ruling themselves. In contrast, the opposition's interpretation of history often perpetuates the myth of the Polish insurrectionist spirit, the Polish inborn love of freedom.

A song composed during the Solidarity strikes reads in part:

> We've got democracy
> won with our father's blood. . . .
> Today we stand firmly
>   by equality,
>   by freedom,
> against the rule of force. . . .
> Stop telling us that we are stupid,
> ungovernable and without experience.

Both camps possess their own ritual language and have developed different terms for the same thing. The opposition claims that the ruling elite "speaks 'Newspeak.' " But the opposition replaces certain terms and phrases used by the ruling elite with its own terms and has itself built a ritual language. The ruling elite calls the U.S.S.R. *Związek Radziecki* (Soviet Union) and avoids using the term *Sowiecki* (Soviet), which has anti-Communist connotations and is regarded by the ruling elite as derogatory. On the other hand, the opposition considers another term, *Radziecki* (Soviet), to be pro-Communist, and it most frequently uses the word *Sowiecki*. Whereas the ruling elite talks of *Komuniści* (Communists), the opposition often talks simply of *Czerwoni* (Reds) or even uses the grammatical singular *Czerwony* (Red), a usage which has become derogatory.

Using the language of one's camp is of utmost importance in the war of rhetoric. If I were closely aligned with the ruling elite, for instance, but used language associated with the opposition, my ruling elite colleagues would question my loyalty.

The two sides demand loyalty from their respective constituencies, shunning those who break the rules. Pan L., who for years occupied a prominent position in the Communist party apparatus, learned the hard way. He resigned from the party in protest of martial law. His behavior indicated that a burden of many years had been lifted from his shoulders. He hoped to be accepted by the opposition, and when he met opposition activists with whom he had formerly spoken only in a stiff, official manner, he greeted them exuberantly. But they did not wish to be friendly with him. One acquaintance explained the reactions of opposition members: "The moral compromises involved in such a career are so great that once a person has chosen it, even if he later gives up his Party membership, he will have difficulties being socially accepted."

The price of betrayal is high, and, by quitting the Party, Pan L. injured his reputation among those of his colleagues who remained in the Party. Choosing to leave the party had major social repercussions and sharply affected his standing with respect to the ruling elite. Moreover, it did not enable him to penetrate the opposition camp.

The less famous a person is and the less of a public image he has to uphold, the more likely he is to move between the two camps. But an individual who is a definite part of one side cannot change to another. A fallen premier, ousted from public life by his colleagues, can never become part of the opposition.

Social pressure has been an effective tool of the opposition. Shortly after the imposition of martial law, underground Solidarity called for a boycott of the official media and government apparatus. Writing articles for the press (except for Church and professional publications), participating in government committees and appearing on television and radio could qualify one as a collaborator and call one's morality into question. Underground representatives compiled a "list of collaborators," containing names of people who had openly endorsed or were suspected of supporting the martial law government. Society was to ostracize those whose names appeared on the list.

A well-known actor, the head of the Communist Party Committee at a major Polish theater, voiced his support of martial law on the evening television news. His name was put on the list of collaborators and the word spread. As a result, during the next performances in which he played a major role, the audience began to clap the moment he appeared on stage. The audience clapped so long that in each performance he had to leave the stage without delivering his lines. The actor soon retired.

Similarly, a famous writer delivered short statements on television supporting martial law. People demonstrated their disapproval by stacking copies of books he had authored on the sidewalk in front of his apartment building. This continued for several months, until the writer ceased all public appearances.

Members of the opposition displayed their rejection of "traitors" by refusing to shake hands. In addition to its literal meaning, "to shake hands" means to offer help. A professor from the intelligentsia social circle was shunned by many of her colleagues at the university because her husband appeared on a television talk show during martial law despite the boycott. Even though the husband expressed views highly critical of the government, the very fact that he participated served to morally disqualify not only him, but also his wife. Many of her colleagues refused to shake hands with her.

Social pressure also created almost instant martyrs and heroes. People championed acts of ingenious defiance. A well-respected journalist who resigned for political reasons when martial law was imposed put an advertisement in *Życie Warszawy*, "Looking for honest work" followed by his last name and telephone number. He became a hero. Many people delighted in his clever poke at the government printed in an official newspaper. The issue of the newspaper was in short supply by the following day, and the story was soon folklore. People were also delighted to learn that, as a result of the ad, the journalist received some 30 job offers, even some from state institutions.

The Church supplied a safe arena for protest. On Good Friday, from morning until late into the night, people solemnly crowded the churches to view exhibits conceived by individual parishes. In Warsaw's Old Town, long lines stretched around blocks and street corners. People took in one exhibit, then continued to the next, until they had made the rounds of all the churches in the vicinity. One church exhibit in 1983 featured, in bold characters encircling a crucified Christ, 1956, 1968, 1970, 1976, and 1981—each the date of political protest against the government. The caption read, "The blood of your brother is crying loudly." Another exhibit displayed a man in prison uniform lying on a cell bed. The emblems of nationalist struggles, the "fighting Poland" sign of the World War II resistance movement and a Solidarity sticker lay around the bed.

Other emblems of protest were in evidence daily. In Warsaw, several crosses of flowers surrounded by hymn-singing women, men and children cropped up in church yards, parking lots and public squares. Elderly women brought flowers in the early morning to remake crosses that were frequently dismantled by police during the night.

Protest has continued into the post-martial law era. The funeral of Grzegorz Przemyk, the 19-year-old boy who died after having been beaten by police in the late spring of 1984, provided yet another opportunity for symbolic protest. Thousands of people attended the funeral mass and the burial; the cemetery was overrun with people and covered with flowers. Voice of America estimated that 30,000 people attended the mass and burial; Polish sources corroborated this figure.

The headmaster of the school Przemyk had attended displayed the school emblem. Scores of his classmates and other pupils from his school were present. It took 15 minutes for groups of them to walk past his grave, each group laying flowers on it. The BBC reported that Przemyk's funeral attracted the largest crowd since the funeral of the popular Cardinal Wyszyński, the "patriarch" of Polish Catholicism in the postwar period.

Many attended the funeral who would not have participated in more open protest. Janusz remarked: "I don't go to Solidarity demonstrations, but I went to the funeral. It is necessary to go to fight tyranny."

The Church organized spiritual as well as material support for the opposition. It kept records on internees and sponsored relief efforts for those in prison. Priests were sometimes allowed into prisons to conduct mass for internees. They delivered supplies and messages to prisoners and, in turn, left with messages and counterfeit materials bulging from their clothes.

The Church also organized support for the opposition community. As every year, in 1982, after the traditional Christmas Eve service held at midnight, young members of the opposition community gathered for a private celebration in a back room of the parish church. Former internees, as well as sons, daughters, husbands, wives, lovers and close friends of those interned and blacklisted—greeted each other with kisses. A priest conducted a short service. "We sang, broke bread together and felt like one family," said a participant.

The Church continues to provide forums for independent activities. Film, plays, art and photography exhibits, which, because of their "anti-state" nature cannot be shown, performed or exhibited elsewhere, find their home in church facilities.

In Poland, many people feel themselves a society unrelated to the apparatus of the state. By general acceptance of citizens, the state is the organized structure that confronts and governs the people who comprise society. Martial law engendered extreme polarization, with the forces of society juxtaposed with those of the state. At the height of tension, Solidarity, the self-appointed representative of society, became a nationalistic, anti-state revivalistic movement. It was like a religious resurrection.

BETWEEN PARTY AND SOLIDARITY

"Politics" impinges on people's lives, inundating the everyday climate, yet it is difficult for a foreigner to uncover its many levels. People socialized into such a system prudently keep us guessing about underlying motives. Adept politicians, they weasel through the maze of competing and coinciding demands which are themselves complicated by constant political upheaval. People's political allegiances are not always clear-cut—they can overlap or change with the situation. Poles use political rhetoric both to obscure and further their vital interests. Behind political rhetoric lie layers of meaning and activity vital to understanding Polish life. While there are "hardcores," most people move back and forth between the extremes and do what they must to survive.

Pan D. was out late one evening, after the 11:00 curfew of the early months of martial law. He wanted to get home but had to avoid being seen by patrolling police who would check his documents and possibly fine him or take him to the police station. He noticed that some buses were still running, probably en route to the bus terminal. Pan D. stood in a dark doorway near a deserted bus stop while he waited for a bus. When one approached, he waved his arms furiously for the driver to stop. He ran to it as fast as he could and jumped in. The bus was dark.

He knelt down and hid between two seats so that his shadow could not be detected. But as the bus passed through well-lit areas of town, he realized he was not alone on his trip home—all around him arms, legs and heads protruded from under the seats.

At one stop, an army officer got on the bus. Pan D. overheard the conversation the officer had with the driver. The officer advised the driver on how to proceed so as not to encounter any difficulties with authorities; he directed the driver to routes that would not have checkpoints that night.

Pan D. struck up a conversation with the officer. The officer asked him if he knew of a comfortable outdoor place to bide his nightlong guard duty. He also asked Pan D. if he had any underground literature with him. "We have difficulties getting such material," he said. So Pan D. pulled out a leaflet from his coat pocket and gave it to the uniformed man, who kindly thanked him.

The army officer's formal identity did not keep him from his own views or private activities. Neither did the official activities of many people I met. I had thought that people belonged either to Solidarity or to the Party, felt strongly about one or the other and participated in the activities of only one. I had thought families and friendships would be divided along those lines. But I soon learned that, in Poland, real political divisions tend to stem not from identification with an ideology or membership in a formal political organization, but from loyalty to a *środowisko* (social circle). The boundary of a given *środowisko* is one of potential and actual informal contacts. Between two different *środowiska*, there is no familial closeness of private relations. Distance between various *środowiska* makes political hatred possible.

Acquaintances of mine, a young married couple with a baby, arranged to exchange their apartment for a similar one in a different district. The transaction was nearly finalized when they learned that some policemen and their families lived in the apartment building in which they wanted to make their home. The acquaintances immediately decided against the move: "Under no circumstances will we open the way for our child to play with children of policemen when she grows up," they said.

On the other hand, I found myself confused when invited to a dinner in the early weeks of martial law and seated with people whose political positions both differed and overlapped. I was invited to one such party by the son of the hostess. Across from me sat a Party member, who, I learned during the conversation, had a son-in-law who had been interned for underground Solidarity activities. Beside me sat a woman, Pani F., who worked in the Communist Party apparatus. She boasted of her daughter, who was "making a career in photography in the United States." And she brought along her boyfriend, a psychiatrist, who talked of the increased number of mental health cases he and his colleagues had seen since martial law.

I had heard rumors that the boyfriend's son was involved in underground activities. He had come that day to the apartment the boyfriend shared with Pani F., bringing an instrument which would determine whether the telephone was bugged.

One Party member complained that he was unable to travel to the Soviet Union, as few Poles were allowed to do so. "These days, Poles can only travel to the West," he lamented. Another party member asked, "But why, for God's sake, would you want to travel to the Soviet Union?" The same man invited me to accompany him to the upcoming May 1st parade and then joked: "Come if you want to see an empire in decline."

A guest boasted of his brother, who was doing well as a private entrepreneur. He turned to me and jokingly urged me to import hot tubs to Poland. "One can make a lot of money doing private business in

Poland." And he added, laughing, "The only question is, would the hot tubs be bugged?" But a guest across the table chimed in, "No. Agents would be standing around with their binoculars instead."

The doorbell rang. A teacher, an acquaintance of the hostess, appeared at the door unexpectedly. Visibly upset, the teacher explained she had done nothing wrong, but that "the whole situation of martial law makes me extremely nervous." The hostess offered her a drink to calm her nerves and insisted she join the other guests at the table. The teacher said, "What they're doing is terrible. I hate the Party, and I hate the government." None of the guests hurried to defend either.

Almost everyone present at the dinner, except myself, expressed anti-government views. Yet most were or had formerly been connected with the Party. All had family members and friends "on the other side." And all would consider themselves and their families part of the same *środowisko*.

Overlapping affiliations and allegiances that seem contradictory to an outsider abound in Poland. To the distant observer there appears a conflict in the fact that a person can write for the official press and, at the same time, author articles for the underground. Yet in the Polish context this is not an uncommon occurrence. To the distant observer it seems a contradiction that one family member could be a Party apparatchik while another could be a Solidarity activist. Yet this, too, is not uncommon, and such varying affiliations by no means ensure that relations will be strained.

In the liberalization that accompanied the Solidarity period, overlapping afiliations were entirely commonplace. Considerable overlap in Solidarity and Communist Party memberships existed. About 20 percent of the delegates elected to the Party Congress of July 1981, mostly rank and file, were members of Solidarity. Roughly one-third of the Communist Party's three million members at some point during this period belonged to Solidarity. But then blatant dual affiliation became more subtle, and many dropped out of the Party.

According to the Central Statistical Office, there was a constant rate of decline in Party membership after the birth of Solidarity and continuing through martial law. Membership dropped by one-third; seven times fewer candidates or recruits joined the Party in 1983 as compared to 1980. The difference between the rates of decline could be explained by the fact that, while it is difficult to give up Party membership, which may jeopardize long-standing privileges and connections, it is easy not to join.

The imposition of martial law created an extreme polarization between Solidarity, now forced underground on one side, and the government of General Jaruzelski and its apparatus on the other. The one-third of Party members who either relinquished their membership or were expelled from the Party was approximately the same percentage that had belonged to both Solidarity and the Party. Though dual membership is less acceptable now than it was when Solidarity was a legal organization, dual participation did not end when Solidarity was outlawed. Even during the most polarized period of martial law, Party member Pan H., who never belonged to Solidarity, often successfully served as an advocate for colleagues at his university who had been arrested or interned.

The Polish system encourages individuals to manipulate the presentation of their allegiances to promote economic and other family-based purposes. It encourages them to expand their affiliations—to learn to know more individuals on a private basis, to associate themselves with more informal organizations, to get their foot in the door of more *środowiska*. Poles have more chances to get what they need if they have their fingers in several political pies. The

strategic use of presentations is importantly woven
into the fabric of Polish life.

Official identities are labels, guaranteeing only that
people will engage in specific activities and self-presentations at certain times. Pan H. and Pan G. are
friends. They are academics working at affiliated research institutes. Both were Party members and were
seen at Party events together, yet Pan H. served as
an advisor to Solidarity during the negotiations of
1980 in Gdańsk, while Pan G. was an advisor to the
government in the same negotiations. Both served
as mediators.

In settings such as Party meetings, participants use
official "Newspeak." They must be prepared to pay
lip service to Marxist-Leninist ideology, just as
American politicians are obliged to espouse a belief
in God regardless of whether they believe. Few Party
members are driven by ideological vision, as one acknowledged:

> When I joined the Party, most Party members in the
> university *środowisko* grappled with Marxist-Leninist the-
> ory. This ended in the mid-1960s. Thereafter, only a few
> continued to be concerned with ideological issues.
> I think that you can find among the Party membership
> all possible political views, just as among non-Party mem-
> bers you can find all possible political positions. It is not
> possible to say that people in the Party are close to me in
> every respect. I would say that these people are differen-
> tiated in a lot of different respects, as well as in political
> matters. It's paradoxical, but it's true. In Poland, the di-
> vision into Party and non-Party is, to a large extent, a di-
> vision without much meaning.

The same Party member described opportunities
he believes motivates some to join the party: "If
someone wants to be actively involved in various
spheres of public life, political or economic, belonging to the Party is a factor that opens up doors."

Formal identities are often smoke screens enabling
people to serve as brokers for those they choose to

help or protect. Pan B., a former member of the Communist party, used his connections to get his nephew released from prison when he was arrested for his role in the underground Solidarity press. Pan B. manipulates certain connections in military, police and government circles in order to accomplish whatever he needs to have done. To each circle he presents himself as an insider.

Pan B. shifts his political self-presentations depending on who he talks to and the impressions to be made. But he is not a blatant opportunist; rather he handles difficulties with humor, diplomacy and circumspection, and he survives well in unstable Poland. Strategic presentations of political affiliation help families to achieve domestic needs in obtaining many services and jobs.

Pan H. served on one of Jaruzelski's advisory councils yet refused to allow his article to be published in the official press unless martial law was suspended. He explained his refusal as "a psychological thing that surprised even me." He added, "To be on either side of the political fence is crazy and to be in the middle is to collaborate. So what can one do in this situation?"

A professional woman attending a conference in the United States when martial law was declared decided to stay in the U.S. indefinitely. In Poland she had neither been interested in politics nor had she flirted with any political activities or organization, legal or illegal. She asked her best friend's husband, a martial law government official, to arrange to renew her Polish passport, and, for several years, he did so. But the husband died unexpectedly, and she could no longer rely on him. Wishing to continue her career in the United States, she claimed to be a member of the underground and sought political asylum in the U.S. Some Polish friends were shocked by her actions, but for her, this was a "normal" way to solve the problem.

While one can understand that Communist Party members might defend colleagues, friends and family members, less explicable for Westerners is the involvement of some Party members in "anti-government" political organizations. People demonstrate their allegiance to the opposition through contributions of goods, services or money, rather than through formal membership. An active member of the Communist Party has belonged to Solidarity since its beginning. Despite the formal prohibition of Solidarity, he continues to pay his Solidarity dues, now secretly.

One way in which people with differing political affiliations overlap is in their religious activities. In a country in which nearly 95 percent of the population is Catholic, it is difficult to imagine that there could be a mass organization whose members were totally uninvolved in church activities. Indeed, many Communist Party members and many members of the ruling elite publicly or privately participate in the activities of the Catholic Church or are affiliated with it in some way. A man who made his career in the Communist Party apparatus calls himself a "believer" and claims that 70 percent of Communist Party members attend church. A member of the Polish Union of Socialist Youth claims that 80 percent of the members of his young peoples' socialist organization are practicing Catholics.

While interned during martial law, Jan received a postcard from the wife of a Communist Party official. The card read as follows:

> Dear Jan,
>   With Resurrection Day coming, the holiday meaning so much to us Catholics, I and my family wish you and your friends [fellow internees] all the best. We do and will accompany all of you with our very, very tender thoughts.

In Poland personal allegiances generally overshadow political loyalties, and loyalty to family is foremost among these personal concerns. Networks of family and friends provide essential social and economic security in uncertain times. They are a way of insuring the future as much as possible. Loyalty to one's *środowiska* often overrides allegiance to any organization or institution, whether the Party, the Church or Solidarity. "We can't risk family life and our unity for politics," explains one Pole. "In private family life, the problem of politics can't exist. This problem exists in public life: in jobs, in the office, at Party and organizational meetings."

The Solidarity movement gave rise to ideological conflict between generations. Generally, more younger people participated than older ones. When Solidarity went underground with the imposition of martial law, those who became active in the underground were almost exclusively of the younger generation. Pani Janina, a survivor of two major 20th-century wars, encouraged her children and grandchildren to be cautious, expressing opinions such as: "If you go too far, we will have a real *regime* in Poland. You don't know what a regime is, what Stalinism is. What do you want—to have no freedom and no hope for liberalization at all? . . . If I had been in your position after the war, I would have been very happy. You have many things I didn't have then—television, refrigerators, work."

Many young adults in their twenties are dependent on their parents, but no one is dependent on them in turn. They are protected and have guaranteed shelter; they live and eat at home. If they lose their jobs, parents will likely provide for them; they may, in fact, be protected from harm by family connections. The Party member who invited me to march with him in an official May Day parade told me later, almost proudly, that his daughter was picked up by police at an illegal Solidarity demonstration on the same day. I learned through other sources that the police let the daughter go after she told them who her father was.

Family unity usually transcends political disagreements. One often finds family members with varying political affiliations, but rarely do they sever their ties because of political disputes. Regardless of how different their political views or affiliations may be, family members typically accept their obligations towards each other.

Tomek, the son of a former high-ranking government official ousted because of pressure from Solidarity when it came into existence, actually worked for Solidarity himself. The son maintained close relations with his family through the entire crisis—the Solidarity and martial law periods—when his family was ostracized by almost everyone, including Solidarity, the underground and the current government. The subject of politics is taboo in Tomek's household.

Yet, even for Tomek, identity as a member of a ruling elite family will continue to be central. Though differing political affiliations can coexist within such a family, identity as a member of the ruling elite is permanent. Belonging to an opposition or a ruling elite family tends to overshadow whatever private activities a family member participates in. No matter what underground involvements Tomek might have, few would believe that he is seriously engaged in such activities. No matter what Tomek does or says privately, people will continue to associate him with the reputation of his father. If he marries someone from a different *środowisko,* she may be stigmatized by the association with the former official.

The son of a famous Stalinist changed his name to avoid having to deal with the negative association. Yet the stigma was passed on even to his child, who became known as the grandson of the famous Stalinist. The grandson married a woman from the traditional intelligentsia *środowisko.* The mother of the bride was most upset about the marriage. "He could have been a drunk, he could have been uncultured, but the grandson of _____?"

Many children of high-ranking officials are in fact apolitical. It is their only recourse if their personal views differ or if they wish to be socially acceptable to *środowiska* not associated with the ruling elite. As Deputy Prime Minister, Mieczysław Rakowski, whose children emigrated to the West, was often asked by workers during his visits to factories, "If you can't raise your children properly, how can you rule the country?" Family members of high-ranking ruling elites, as well as of opposition leaders, have permanent identities as such. Without respect to their own views or affiliations, they will be known as the son or daughter or wife of the famous person.

The consequences of having a particular identity or reputation are often unpredictable, leaving people with few guidelines as to how to act. Sometimes it is difficult to know from day to day which individuals or group of individuals will be denounced as collaborators, as irrational Solidarity extremists, or as "hard heads." It is difficult to know which activities will be seen as dangerous and which will be tolerated.

Though one might expect repression in an East European country to follow underground activities, sanctions are often haphazardly applied. One young activist remarked, "Poland is a crazy country. The system is set up to *not* be predictable. It is designed to control through harassment; dependent people should be afraid, but most will not be punished."

Having been a key figure in Solidarity, Maria's husband seemed a likely candidate for arrest when martial law was declared. On a bright sunny day in the early months of martial law, I had coffee with Maria, a young professional. Talking in a hushed voice in a cafe in Cracow's Old Town, Maria nervously related the latest political rumors and speculated about the future of her acquaintances in "political trouble." Walking through the cobblestoned streets of the city, she talked more specifically about her own situation. To escape possible arrest, Maria and her husband went into hiding immediately after martial law was declared. Moving from house to house and staying with co-conspirators in chilly, cramped quarters in the dead of winter, they eluded the police, only to discover that the police had never pursued them. It is difficult for many to predict accurately the consequences of their actions, and this makes them insecure.

A professor at the university generously offered me his wife's help. A well-placed official in a government office, she could get unpublished statistics that he thought would broaden my research base. I had not solicited the wife's assistance—the husband had volunteered her help. Yet shortly thereafter, American-Polish relations took a dramatic turn for the worse. The husband came to me apologetically several weeks later after subtly hedging the issue several times and said, "My wife could have an unpleasant experience if she allows you to see the research findings at this time."

In the midst of a vacillating political situation, official identities and public reputations change. Former premiers become nobodies, too embarrassed to go out in public. Low-level Solidarity workers, formerly unknown, are elevated to the status of national heroes. Everyone—Communist Party members, government officials, Solidarity activists, General Jaruzelski's advisors and cabinet members, Lech Wałęsa, Solidarity leaders and even General Jaruzelski himself—is on the political fence. And because what is really going on can be verified only by the grapevine, the present is ambiguous, the future even more uncertain.

The uncertainty makes it difficult for those inside and outside the country to grasp Polish politics. Poles cannot be sure how their past and present activities and affiliations will be regarded in the future. One activist was upset by the "carelessness" of her colleagues working in the underground. She pleaded with them not to leave obvious trails for police when meeting with co-conspirators in supposedly secret locations. She warned them that things can change overnight: "What is seen as careful behavior today may be considered careless behavior tomorrow."

7

An Eye
on the Future

What will the future hold for the millions of babies born during the recent baby boom in Poland? As Janusz and I sat in a cafe several days before I left Poland, we talked of stories we heard and games we played as children. "But American and Polish children born today will not have many childhood experiences in common," he said. "Computers and videogames will be the toys of American children. For Polish children, such things will be like a fairy tale."

Poles are not likely to see fundamental changes in their lives in the foreseeable future. One thing, however, is almost certain: As the official economy wavers, the already large gap between the haves—those who have *dojście* and/or considerable money—and the have-nots—will widen. Poles will continue to seek satisfaction through connections which enable them to cope with and adjust to the system. The political climate will vacillate from harassment to accommodation.

It is difficult for everyone—Polish and foreign observers alike—to see beyond Poland's economic crisis. A 1985 article in *Polityka* reads:

> We estimate that in 1983 Poland's aggregate foreign debt reached 55.4 percent and debt in convertible currencies alone 50.3 percent of the gross national income produced. This is a considerable amount, not only in comparison with

some socialist countries, but even in comparison with heavily indebted Third World nations.

With a $30 billion debt to Western commercial creditors and a complicated set of Warsaw Pact economic and political constraints, the country's rulers will continue for some time to be engaged in a delicate balancing act. According to *Polityka*, in 1983 alone, the interest on the debt amounted to $2.1 billion, or 39 percent of revenue from Polish exports to hard-currency countries. As the Deputy Finance Minister acknowledged: "We should reconcile ourselves to the fact that for several years ahead, despite growth in convertible exports, our debt will be on the increase." Foreign debt and domestic defence spending burdens will encumber all future policy making.

For the Warsaw Pact powers, the imposition of martial law was a long-needed measure that reasserted Eastern Bloc constraints. For the West, the imposition of martial law in 1982 was a blight on Poland. Ensuing economic sanctions from the United States and West European countries blocked further assistance from foreign creditors and dashed hope for immediate membership in the International Monetary Fund and the World Bank, leaving Poland's prospects for fulfilling its debt obligations even bleaker. The West has since agreed to debt rescheduling and the prospect of IMF membership. Nevertheless, reports in the official press predict that, by the year 2000, the Polish debt could be as high as $100 billion.

Consumers will continue to buy Polish chicken in West Berlin and Polish leather goods in Paris; the goods are in short supply in Poland and are exported to the West for hard currency. British homes will continue to be heated by Polish coal. Revenues from these exports will help to pay off the interest on the debt. But the defaulting and "rescheduling" of loans has already begun. However low their pro-

ity, Polish workers will see the fruits of their
ported for years to come while their working
and living standards decline.

rmoil, bred in part by economic hard-
w for years until it erupts again, as it
se of Solidarity in 1980. In the wake
Soviet leaders Leonid Brezhnev, Yuri
onstantin Chernenko, Poles invari-
bout the fate of their nation. But
ted considerable change.

es of the opposition will find expression both
underground and public forums. The seesaw of
Warsaw Pact constraints and the challenge to those
constraints will outline the immediate future. As the
opposition continues to mobilize its resources, forces
of repression will in turn mobilize theirs. Opposition
leader, Adam Michnik, wrote from his Gdańsk prison
cell, in an essay printed in the *New York Review of
Books*, the following:

> Poland continues to be what it was: a country where
> the nation strives for freedom and autonomy, and the au-
> thorities try to force it back into a totalitarian corset. . . .
> repression leads the government into a blind alley . . .
>   Yes, it is possible to govern in this way. So long as geo-
> politics is favorable, this system may last for quite some
> time.

Poland's ongoing troubles—the catch-all "crisis"
credited by many parties for being both cause and
symptom of practically anything that goes wrong—
will by no means disappear. Long-standing problems, including environmental ones, will compound
Poland's predicament. A 1985 article in *Życie Warszawy* reports that Poland is the most environmentally polluted country in Europe. According to a study
conducted by the Polish Academy of Sciences, the
growing incidence of cancer and other serious dis-
eases in Poland is due mainly to the contamination
of food, water and the atmosphere.

Chronic crisis can be reasonably forecast. Still more uncertainty will result in more social problems: Alcoholism and other substance abuse will likely increase, along with the suicide rate. A society pays for unfulfilled hope: In 1980—the period of Solidarity—the suicide rate dropped by 70 percent from the previous year. But it has increased by 70 percent since 1981.

Still more uncertainty will lend renewed credence to the spiritual realm: *Duchowe* life will thrive, as will already entrenched notions of human destiny and fate. Movements towards a social utopia, based on Polish-style Catholicism, will likely gain prominence.

Fundamentally, the overall system will remain as it is; those who operate within it will carry on as they have been. As acknowledged by sources published in the official press, the system of private arrangements is in Poland to stay. In a 1984 article in *Polityka*, economist Jerzy Kleer speculated about the future of the Polish "parallel economy":

> The present peculiar circumstances shape the image of the Polish parallel economy. . . . Developing services could change a lot. However, we must not delude ourselves that the parallel economy can be totally eliminated or that intensified control would be sufficient. We must counteract the parallel economy; however, it is unreasonable to expect great success.

Though the facts may change, the way people cope with them will remain constant. People will consciously try to privatize their relationships and to make one relationship fulfill many functions. They will make private arrangements either through connections or through an elaborate and time-consuming etiquette of exchange. They will play their own small parts in the informal economy, which inevitably will adjust to the vagaries of the official distribution system. It will be awhile before Barbara's

mother will need to *załatwić* another pass for her
nephew so he can "see his grandfather for the last
time," but she will need other things, and she will
help Barbara to acquire the things she will require
when she has a family. Ala will keep on exchanging
goods and information with her country cousins and
small town friends; Pani R. will make arrangements
with the laundry woman and will earn the good
graces of store clerks through flattery.

* * *

Informal channels or solutions often come into play
as people try to acquire scarce goods or services. The
formal system promotes the development of an informal economy when informal channels are the only
means to a desired good, service, benefit or privilege
or when informal channels are simply easier than
formal channels. Informal activities flourish where
people have learned that working around the rules
is the only, or most desirable, way of meeting their
needs.

Under certain circumstances, such as the existence
of price controls and administrative rationing of goods
found in many East European and developing countries, informal economies are a mainstay for societies
facing declining standards of living. Black market
dealing and pooling of familial resources, both within
and between countries, often enables people to survive. A lack of desired goods and services can con-
vert informal relations into concrete problem-solving
operations.

Observers of life in Poland often wonder why public
authorities permit widespread informal economic exchange. Outsiders wonder why a government that
was able to impose martial law so efficiently is unable to quash the system of private arrangements.

Indeed, in Poland as in many East European
countries, many informal economic activities are in

fact stimulated by the relevant public authorities. In such countries, the official and the informal economies are so completely intertwined that it is impossible to speak of their practical operation separately.

Several complementary reasons help explain why the formal structure, which would seem to oppose the informal structure, in practice usually works in tandem with it. The dependency of the bureaucracy on informal ways and means is embedded in the overall structure of the bureaucratic system and can be seen in specific policy decisions. To finance the state economy, for instance, the Polish government encourages citizens to spend dollars—often illegally acquired—in its Pewex stores. And it depends heavily on monies produced by private legal enterprises, the operation of which usually involves illegal activities.

The pervasive system of private arrangements is useful to the state in yet another way. Private arrangements satisfy consumers at times when state resources are unable to do so. That the basic needs of a populace be fulfilled is critical in maintaining stability in a country in which the faith of the people in their government has long been, at best, in question, and in which the state is seen in stark contrast to society. The existence of a second, informal system helps minimize potential popular discontent due to the fundamental difficulty of economic reforms, impossible to separate from political reforms.

While certain informal economic activities find their source in uniquely Polish circumstances, others arise from a set of economic restraints that might be found in other traditions. One friend expressed the dilemma that puzzles many, "Poland isn't a Third World country, and yet, in many ways, it is." The system of private arrangements calls to mind the economy of a less developed nation.

Some of the informal mechanisms and responses I observed in Poland derive directly from Polish history and traditional culture. Established patterns tend to linger on unless the conditions which encouraged their development change. Features which set Poland apart from other East European countries include a tradition of "peasant family economy," in which privately-owned land is cultivated and kept within a family, a history of extralegal networking and resistance refined through centuries of foreign rule and the important social and political role played by the Catholic Church. These elements have combined to empower people with more independence from state institutions and enable them to operate yet more extensively outside of the state system.

Conclusions drawn about the context in which Poland's informal economy has arisen and its connections to government and social systems provide insight into other societies with a similar informal economy. Increasing attention is being given to "second," "parallel," "underground," "shadow" and "black" economies around the world, and assertions are being made about their growth, pervasive nature and interrelationships to political and social systems. Indeed, geographically and culturally diverse societies, historic and contemporary, provide examples of informal economic activity and organization. Social scientists have documented informal economies not only in Latin America, Asia, Africa, the Soviet Union and Eastern Europe but also in Western Europe and the United States.

Recent study indicates widespread informal economic activity in many African nations—among them Uganda, Zaire, Ghana and the length and breadth of Third World nations. In China, for example, the exchange of favors underlying informal economic transactions is called *guanxi*. In Chile the middle class participates in a system of favors and friendships called *compadrazgo*.

The informal economic activity described in Poland exists in some form in the Soviet Union and in all East European countries, where many individual problem-solving strategies are grounded not in formal procedures but in social networks which circumvent such procedures. Informal economies have arisen as well in the non-Slavic East European countries of Hungary, Romania and East Germany. The appearance in East Germany of moonlighting, black market trade in hard currencies and other informal economic developments similar to those found in Poland indicates that the postwar system has stimulated them.

Though many examples of informal economic activity can be found around the world, it is important that they should be understood within the context in which they thrive. Similar activities do not always achieve comparable functions or have like meanings.

Borrowing butter from one's neighbor is an informal social exchange, regardless of which society it occurs in. However, if I borrow butter from my neighbor in the United States, it usually has a different meaning than if I borrow butter from my neighbor in Poland. If I am a middle or upper-class American living in the United States, the fact that my neighbor is kind enough to lend me butter saves me a trip in my car to the supermarket. If my neighbor lends me butter in Poland, however, he will probably go without his monthly ration. Borrowing butter from my neighbor in the United States does not require a meaningful relationship; at worst, it is simply a nuisance for the parties concerned. However, in Poland, because butter is a desired item, defined as scarce, it is tied to intimate relationships. One does not give away butter to a mere acquaintance. The private exchange of butter is so highly valued that it is reserved for the most intimate and long-term relationships.

Though informal systems exist in many societies, the ways in which people view them vary from society to society. Poles acknowledge that the informal economy is very important in Poland. Though certain informal economic activities can be found in the United States, many Americans, accustomed to the ideals of "bureaucratic rationality," would negate their importance and prevalence. There is a greater dichotomy between official Polish socialist ideology and the prevalence of informal economic activities than there is between free-enterprise ideology and life for most middle and upper-class Americans. For this group of Americans, humiliation is not, as it often is in Poland, a main feature of dealing with formal structures in the pursuit of a "normal" life.

In situations of scarcity, it has often come as a surprise that people fared better than expected. Official projections are often inaccurate because they do not account for the workings of the informal economy. Anthropologist Janet MacGaffey observes that "in countries where the second economy is very large, official figures bear little relation to what is actually going on." MacGaffey's observation strikingly illustrates the importance of knowledge on informal economies to the assessment of "development," which is typically equated with economic growth reflected in official government figures. Reliance only on official figures, in a context that includes a large informal economy, may lead to distorted projections.

The status of informal economies in Poland and in societies around the world has important public policy ramifications for governments, banks and agencies concerned with loans, international aid and development in these countries. Analysis of private economic activity is critical in our projection of future trends in productivity, living standards and economic fluctuation. Informal exchange not only permeates economies but also has a significant influence on the development of political and social aspects of society. Without an understanding of the internal distribution and redistribution mechanisms

of informal economic systems and a grasp of how
external constraints in the form of economic policies
impinge on local economies, the effects of such policies may not be the intended ones.

* * *

Forty years after World War II, I asked Polish
friends and acquaintances to comment on what they
thought the next 40 years would be like. Though
people reflected over the last 40 years easily, many
reacted to my question about the future with bewil-
derment: "The next 40 years? . . . 40 years . . . ? ?"
The private struggle to survive within a limiting
official system has nurtured both hope and despair.
Everyday life tests the limits of the Polish people;
many I encountered seemed rarely to think about the
future.
I asked Barbara how she sees Poland's present and
future:

> In the United States, Soviet Union and Europe in gen-
> eral, everyone is arming themselves and talking of war.
> . . . I never think about it. It's a thought too far away.
> You know, at the moment I have my own problems here—
> how to get an apartment, how to furnish it when I get it,
> what to wear as a wedding dress—and not whether war
> will break out. I don't reach out for such far thoughts.
> . . . We are accustomed to the situation in Poland, so, for
> us, it is only a thought that somewhere in the world peo-
> ple have it well, have it comfortably, as you know. But in
> everyday life one thinks everyday thoughts, and we are
> simply used to it. It's worse for you. You come from an-
> other world.

For many the future is next week or possibly next
month. Pale, expressionless women ride crammed
buses and trams, resolutely work full shifts at state
jobs, *załatwiają* the shopping and run the household.
They have little time to contemplate the future, other
than how they will get an extra ration of meat next

month. An ever-increasing response is: "Things could get worse."

For some the future lies outside of Poland. Thinking about his students of the last 10 years, a prominent professor remarked, "My most intelligent students have left Poland." But a student who languished seven months in martial law internment told me, "One thing I'm sure of is that I don't want to emigrate. There is a lot to be done on the social level in this country—like changing the educational system, changing life aspirations of people and changing the way people relate to one another. I feel there are a lot of things to do on different levels, and I think I would feel very lonely in the West—in Europe or in the States."

Asking what the future holds is like asking about "the mood in Poland." Everyone has a different answer. There are those who attacked Solidarity as "CIA-inspired." Others said they despised the "Soviet-controlled regime" of General Jaruzelski. Discussion of the future inevitably raised questions about the past, inextricably linked with war, hardship and suffering. "There will be a war," was a comment heard often.

In their reactions to the American film, "The Day After," shown on Polish television, Poles compared their national experience with that of Americans—an experience which inevitably foreshadows the future. Pani R. commented, "The film didn't make an impression on me. The total destruction of Warsaw in 1944 was much more horrible than the destruction portrayed in the film. The film was child's play."

A student at Warsaw University told me, "I definitely didn't like the film. It was not at all realistic—Americans never had a war on their own territory. In times of war, people try to explain who is guilty—they would want to know just who pressed the button. My parents told me that in 1939 [when Hitler's army marched into Poland] people asked each other,

'How could it have come to this? Why is it that we are no longer independent?' In the film it seemed that God had dropped the bomb. It did not show people trying to make moral sense out of their miserable predicaments."

Pani Janina told me, in a pleading tone, "I only hope one thing: that there won't be a war. That would mean the destruction of the world. We pass away anyway—everyday, it seems, one of my acquaintances dies. But why shouldn't you have the chance to live? Why should growing children have to be lost? That is horrible."

A younger person, the 31-year-old son of an army officer said, "There will be a war. The third war. If there isn't a war, I predict that it will be very difficult in the world from an economic standpoint. The situation of people in the world will worsen, especially here. If the crisis were big enough, the Soviet empire would crumble. Before the year 2000, there is a chance that there will be a war between communism and capitalism."

When asked about his personal future, the same young man, who faces a 10-year wait for his own apartment, replied, "It's dark. Hopeless. I'll tell you openly. In socialism you wait and wait. Only later do you find what you've been waiting for. And I don't see any way out of the situation. That is the worst."

An elderly taxi driver volunteered his prognosis: "It will get worse here. Young people want dollars to come from the sky so they can buy in Pewex. But they don't want to work for it. And those who work at state jobs—honestly—don't have anything to show for their work."

A few, those tirelessly devoted to underground duties, still speak as if they are submerged in another world, where opposition and resistance are uncompromising. "I intend to work towards overthrowing the present political system and creating something new. I'm talking about revolution. . . . I don't see myself as setting fire to police stations—or maybe I will. My role in the revolution is being in prison. If a revolution of this sort comes, I'm sure I'll be in prison, or I'll be organizing groups of people." But few Poles today would rally to such extremist resolve.

A renowned Polish film director, when asked about the current situation, reminisced about past repressions. He spoke of the 1950s when anything Western—Coca-Cola, jazz—was forbidden. He told of Stalinist times, of listening to a group of jazz musicians that played underground. Ten months after the imposition of martial law, the director commented, "No matter how bad things may look, Poland has not returned to the period of Stalinist terror."

The middle-aged son of a famous Stalinist told me, "Young people were much more courageous than older people during Solidarity times. But now many of those young people lack the courage necessary to carry on and are without hope. Older people have previously survived such disappointments and are better equipped to deal with this one."

"It is necessary to survive the crisis," Pani R. shrugged, laughing as she swallowed her straight-up vodka. "Look at the Israelis. Forty years after the Second World War, Poles are still scrambling around for eggs. The Israelis have eggs, and they sell them as well." A concentration camp survivor, Pani R. concluded, "A person can adjust to anything."

In a *Wall Street Journal* article from June of 1985, Deputy Premier Mieczysław Rakowski talks about the future of the Polish system.

> Commenting on an unreleased, semiofficial report calling for substantial changes in socialism, he says, "It's true that socialism must change. At this point it is difficult to tell what the changes will be in 10 years' time. For example, the French revolution was victorious in 1792. Before the capitalist system evolved out of that revolution, it had

to take over 100 years . . . for a system to find a new kind of image takes decades."

Opposition leader Adam Michnik has a different view. Writing for the *New York Review of Books,* he exhorts the authorities and refers specifically to Generals Jaruzelski and Kiszczak (Minister of Internal Affairs):

> They are much too confident. They forget that the sociology of surprise is hidden in the nature of the leading system. Here, on a spring morning, one may wake up in a totally changed country. Here, and not once, Party buildings burned while the commissars escaped clad only in their underwear. Edward Gierek, so beloved by Brezhnev and Helmut Schmidt, so respected by Giscard d'Estaing and Carter, within a week travelled from the heights of power into oblivion. *Sic transit gloria mundi.*

In a welcoming address to the Pope during his 1983 visit to martial law Poland, General Jaruzelski proclaimed:

> But today we want to look above all forward to the future, to a better tomorrow for Poland. We have undertaken resolutely the cause of reforms. The renewal in social, state, economic life becomes legally and factually irreversible. The moral health of the nation, the fight against faults and wrongdoing, care for youth, family, mother and child lie deep in our heart.
>
> Daily life is difficult. We are grappling with adversities. There are severe human sore spots. There is still much resentment and bitterness. But we have survived the worst. The country has embarked on the road towards the better. Our society can rise with its thought above today's divisions and perplexities. Every day it gives evidence of patriotic responsibility and sacrifice.

Professor of Economics Edward Lipiński, now in his late nineties and the famous grandfather of the Polish opposition, has an unusual vantage point on the past from which to look upon the future. He joined the Polish Socialist Party in 1905 and was 25 years old when World War I broke out. In a meeting in a private home, he offered me a bleak forecast of Poland's future. "Dark," he said slowly, "dark, dark."

Twenty-seven-year-old Dorota was weary of despair. "If you show any optimism at all among my friends, they are *hostile*," she told me. "You are supposed to be depressed, to say everything is bad and that nothing will work out and not to look forward to the future. It's popular to be pessimistic."

Thinking back on my own impressions of martial law Poland, I was torn. Life was sometimes truly joyful, other times intensely frustrating and still others overwhelmingly oppressive. The everyday atmosphere—that of cramped quarters, greasy meat in dismal state restaurants, blank-faced people standing in line—was pervaded by a creeping dullness. "There's a lot that's enormously dull here," remarked a friend. "Nothing happens most of the time."

Yet there is *duchowe* life to break the monotony, and I missed its richness when my stay in Poland was over. In Poland not only do people need each other for bread-and-butter but also for private *duchowe* living—the sharing of one's own predicament—that they create together. When two policemen out shopping asked me how I liked Poland, I gave a safe and truthful answer, "I like Poles very much."

When I left in 1986, the air was still rife with political rumor and goose stepping soldiers. Yet things seemed much more relaxed and "normal" than they had when I first arrived in 1982. The market situation had greatly improved. Lines for goods and services were far less frequent and shorter; at the same time, prices for many goods had risen substantially.

The atmosphere of constant edginess among the people was gone, replaced in many by stoic or bitter resentment. Two years after the imposition of martial law, Barbara talked of changes since its early days:

The moment of the announcement [of martial law] was a horrible experience for me. I didn't know exactly what was going on. Such confusion—some kind of vehicle, here soldiers, there police drove; everyone wondered what it was about and what had happened. You know, it was terrible. But now, all in all, one can get used to everything, so somehow I have got used to it. It seems to me that things are already better. In addition to that, there is no longer martial law. Things are a little more normal.

Several months after he was released from prison, one activist, clad in jeans and a flannel shirt, told me, "It all seems very far away now." His lips and hands trembled as he chain smoked. "After two months, I haven't forgotten it on a feeling level; I still can *feel* it, but when I talk about it, it's like I'm reading a book of . . . second-hand memories."

For me the stress and tedium was interrupted by the humor of friends, by the amusing contradictions which crop up in everyday life—the policemen who harass me, yet want me to help them pick out perfume; the policewoman who insists on repeating black market prices on the telephone; the finagling of Barbara's mother as she arranges a date for me with Barbara's cousin in the army; the Party member who invites me to come to the official May 1st parade if I want to see "the Party in decline." The tedium was also interrupted by confusion and fear—occasional police surveillance, a strip-search, an aggressive official anti-American campaign, moments when underground workers tried to involve me in illegal activities, which I, an observer, felt I must refuse to participate in.

Janusz summed up the prevailing mood, "Most people are coming to the point where they just want to be left alone. Young people just want to get married and have a family right away. People are tired of trouble and of struggle. They simply want peace. Such is life."

pplementary Sources

Jerzy. "How Much for a Dollar?" *Polityka-Ex-rt* (August 1984). Polish News Bulletin translations, with free constructions by author based on original Polish text.

Bednarski, Marek. "Drugi Obieg" [Second Circulation]. *Życie Gospodarcze* (26 August 1984): 35.

Beskid, Lidia, ed. *Warunki Życia i Potrzeby Społeczeństwa Polskiego 1982 [Living Conditions and Needs of Polish Society: 1982]*. Warszawa: Polska Akademia Nauk, Instytut Filozofii i Sociologii, 1984.

Ciągłość i Zmiana Tradycji Kulturowej. [Continuity and Change of Cultural Tradition] Volumes I and II. Prepared for internal use by the Group of Methodological Sociological Research (Zakład Metodologii Badań Socjologicznych Uniwersytet Warszawski) July 1976.

Curry, Jane. *The Black Book of Polish Censorship.* New York: Random House, 1984.

Davies, Norman. "The Making of His Mind, Review of *The Land of Ulro* by Czesław Miłosz." *The New York Times Book Review* (2 September 1984).

Davies, Norman. *God's Playground: A History of Poland in Two Volumes.* Volume II: *1795 to the Present.* New York: Columbia University Press, 1984.

Dodziuk-Lityńska, Anna and Markowska, Danuta. *Współczesna Rodzina w Polsce* [The Contemporary Family in Poland]. Warszawa: Książka i Wiedza.

Dyczewski, Leon. *Więź Pokoleń w Rodzinie* [Inter-generational Ties Within a Family]. Warszawa: Wydawnictwo Osrodka Dokumentacji i Studiów Społecznych, 1976.

Gross, Jan Tomasz. *Polish Society Under German Occupation: The Generalgouvernement, 1939–1944*. Princeton, New Jersey: Princeton University Press, 1976.

Grossman, Gregory. "The 'Second Economy' of the USSR." *Problems of Communism* 26, No. 5 (September-October 1977): 25–40.

Jarosz, Maria. *Nierówności Społeczne* [Social Inequality]. Warszawa: Książka i Wiedza, 1984.

Kleer, Jerzy. "Parallel Economy in the Shadows." *Polityka* 49 (8 December 1984): 1. Polish News Bulletin translations, with free constructions by author based on original Polish text.

Korbonski, Andrzej. "The 'Second Economy' in Poland." *Journal of International Affairs* 35 (Spring–Summer 1981): 1–15.

Kurczewski, Jacek, ed. *Umowa o Kartki* [(Social) Contract About Ration Cards]. Uniwersytet Warszawski: Instytut Profilaktyki Społecznej i Resocjalizacji, 1985.

Łączkowska, Maria. *Wielkomiejska Rodzina Inteligencka* [Intelligentsia Families in Large Cities]. Poznan: Uniwersytet LL. Adama Mickiewicza: Seria Socjologia No. 12, 1983.

Los, Maria. "The Unmasking of Corruption in the Polish Renewal." Paper presented at the Annual Convention of the American Association for the Advancement of Slavic Studies. September 1981.

MacGaffey, Janet. "How to Survive and Become Rich Amidst Devastation: The Second Economy in Zaire." *African Affairs* (July 1983): 351–366.

Morawski, Witold, ed. *Demokracja i Gospodarka* [Democracy and Economy]. Uniwersytet Warszawski: Instytut Socjologii, 1983.

Narojek, Winicjusz. *Społeczeństwo Otwartej Rekrutacji. Próba Antropologii Klimatu Stosunków Międzyludzkich* [Society of Open Recruitment. An Anthropological Study of Human Relations in Contemporary Poland]. Warszawa: Państwowe Wydawnictwo Naukowe, 1980.

Nowak, Stefan. "System Wartości Społeczeństwa Polskiego [The Value System of Polish Society]. *Studia Socjologiczne* 4: 75 (1979).

Polska: 1946–1983 [Poland: 1946–1983]. Warszawa: Główny Urząd Statystyczny, 1984.

Rodzina w Świetle Wyników Narodowego Spisu Powszechnego 1978 [The Family in Light of the National Census: 1978]. Warszawa: Główny Urząd Statystyczny, 1981.

Rocznik Statystyczny [Statistical Yearbook]. Warszawa: Główny Urząd Statystyczny, 1985.

Rocznik Statystyczny Kultury [Statistical Yearbook of Culture]. Warszawa: Główny Urząd Statystyczny, 1982.

Tarkowski, Jacek. "Patronage in a Centralized Socialist System: The Case of Poland." *International Political Science Review* 4:4 (1983): 495–518.

Wnuk-Lipiński, Edmund, ed. *Nierówności w Polsce.* [Inequality in Poland.] Warszawa: Polska Akademia Nauk, Instytut Filozofii i Socjologii, 1985.

Wnuk-Lipiński. *Budżet Czasu. Struktura Społeczna. Polityka Społeczna* [Time Budget. Social Structure. Social Policy]. Warszawa: Wydawnictwo Polskiej Akademii Nauk, 1981.

Wyka, Kazimierz. *Życie Na Niby. Pamiętnik Po Klęsce* [Pretending to Live. Memoirs After Defeat]. Kraków: Wydawnictwo Literackie, 1984.

Zdaniewicz, Witold, ed. *Religion and Social Life.* Poznań-Warszawa: Pallottinum, 1983.

Zjawiska Społeczne Lat Siedemdziesiątych [Social Phenomena of the 1970s]. Warszawa: Główny Urząd Statystyczny, 1982.

Życie Warszawy. "The Power of Stereotypes: Interview with Zbigniew Nęcki, Ph.D., Head of the Social Psychology Department at Jagiellonian University." (29–30 September 1984): 3.

Życie Warszawy. "Public Opinion on 40 years of Socialist Poland." (5 December 1984): 2. Polish News Bulletin translations, with free construction by author based on original Polish text.

INDEX